AN AMERICAN
PRAYER BOOK

AN AMERICAN PRAYER BOOK

COMPILED AND EDITED BY

CHRISTOPHER L. WEBBER

MOREHOUSE PUBLISHING

an imprint of
Church Publishing Incorporated
New York   Harrisburg

Morehouse Publishing, 4775 Linglestown Road, Harrisburg, PA 17112

Morehouse Publishing, 445 Fifth Avenue, New York, NY 10016

Morehouse Publishing is an imprint of Church Publishing Incorporated.

Cover design by Amy Davis

Library of Congress Cataloging-in-Publication Data

An American prayer book / compiled and edited by Christopher L. Webber.
    p. cm.
  Includes bibliographical references.
  ISBN 978-0-8192-2332-6 (hardcover)
  1. Prayers. 2. United States – Religion. I. Webber, Christopher.
BL2525.A535 2008
204′.33 – dc22

                                             2008021356

Printed in the United States of America

08   09   10   11   12   13   10 9 8 7 6 5 4 3 2 1

Contents

Part One

PRAYERS
FOR AMERICA

Part Two

PRAYERS FROM
AMERICAN HISTORY

Part Three

PRAYERS FOR
NATIONAL OCCASIONS

Introduction

When the first European settlers came to Jamestown, they brought with them a Chaplain, Robert Hunt, and Captain James Smith recorded that they had "daily prayer morning and evening" through the early days of settlement. When deliberations in the Constitutional Convention seemed to be stalled, Benjamin Franklin suggested that they call in a clergyman to lead them in prayer, and that was done. When Allied armies stood poised for the invasion of Europe to throw off the Nazi tyranny, President Franklin Roosevelt led the nation in a prayer of his own composition. So, again and again, in the history of this country, its leaders and people have turned to God in prayer for guidance and strength.

America is not unique in this. Many nations through human history have drawn on their own religious traditions in a similar way, though perhaps none previously had created such a tradition without an established religion. Nonetheless, the prayers of any people inevitably reflect their own history and challenges and are worth studying for what they tell us about a society and its faith.

To publish a collection of American prayers is not intended to suggest that Americans have any special claim on God's favor, but rather to suggest that Americans have in the past prayed about matters unique to American history and that

1

these prayers are of interest today and may still, in many cases, be of use.

Over the years, Americans have constructed, without any plan, a sort of American Church Year, not in conflict with the traditional Christian Year but supplementing it in ways reflecting our own history and needs. Independence Day celebrates the establishment of the United States as a separate entity; Thanksgiving Day recalls the hardships of our early history; Labor Day reminds us of the achievement of our factories and working people; Martin Luther King's birthday reminds us of the victory of African Americans over the evils of segregation and racial prejudice; Memorial Day reminds us of those who have died for this country; Presidents' Day commemorates those who have served as chief executives. Many of these days are celebrated on an ecumenical basis. They commemorate the events that have made us what we are, for better or worse, and remind us of the vision that has been set before us in the past and the vision that remains to be accomplished. Citizens of other countries have their own history and celebrations. These are ours.

This book brings together three types of American prayers. First, there are prayers for America as a society such as might be used on any Sunday or other time of prayer. Second, there are prayers from the American past that were used at special moments in our history. Third, there are prayers for those special occasions that draw us together: Independence Day, Martin Luther King Jr.'s Birthday, Memorial Day, Labor Day, Thanksgiving Day, and others. This last section is intended to be used either verbatim or modified as those using them might find helpful. The prayers from the other sections might also provide models and useful phrases and suggestions. As an indication of what others might do and to make this book more useful, a few of the historic prayers have been provided both in their original version and in a more contemporary style.

This book is intended to be inclusive. There are prayers from Judaism and Islam as well as Christianity. There are also prayers from a broad spectrum of Christians. Not everyone will be comfortable with all these prayers, and some traditions — those which have been here longest and have relied more generally on written prayers — are better represented than others, but most Americans should find here some prayers that they will be able to use.

Some Christian traditions have made it a point not to use written prayers, and even Christians of the liturgical traditions have made much more use in recent years of spontaneous and unwritten prayer. Thus there is a significant strand of American prayer that can never be included in any book. But even those who rely entirely on extemporaneous prayer may be able to learn from the prayers of others and let them "fertilize" their own prayers.

All people need to pray and each of us has special needs and thanksgivings to be offered in our prayers. So, too, do groups of people, congregations, communities, and nations. These are some of the prayers Americans have offered for this society. May they continue to inspire new prayers and times of prayer as we work together with other societies to overcome national divisions and build a world at peace.

In collecting these prayers I am grateful for the assistance of the Rev. Richard Tabor of the Congregational Church in Salisbury, Connecticut; Rabbi James Perman of Naples, Florida, a friend of many years; Frank Turner and the staff of the Beinecke Library at Yale; Peter Knapp and the staff of the Watkinson Library at Trinity College, Hartford; Karen Lesiak, Library Director of the Archbishop O'Brien

Library in Bloomfield, Connecticut; and the Rt. Rev. Jeffrey Rowthorn.

Some unusual spellings in the prayers (cloathed, labour, to-day, *et al*) are in the original texts. Pronouns referring to God (Thou, He, *et al*) are capitalized or not as in the original version.

Christopher L. Webber
July 4, 2008

PART ONE

Prayers for America

GENERAL PRAYERS
FOR THE COUNTRY

One of the most frequently copied prayers for America was written by the Rev. George Lyman Locke, who served for forty-two years as Rector of St. Michael's Church, Bristol, Rhode Island, and wrote the Prayer for Our Country at the suggestion of the Rev. Daniel Reed Huntington. It was added to the Episcopal Church's Book of Common Prayer in the revision of 1928 and has since been included in the Lutheran Book of Worship, various non-denominational hymnals and prayer books, and even in the prayer book of the Anglican Church in Nigeria. Often revised in various ways, it is given below both in its original form and in the current version from the 1979 Book of Common Prayer.

For Our Country

Almighty God, who in former time leddest our fathers forth into a wealthy place, and didst set our feet in a large room; Give thy grace, we humbly beseech thee, to us their children, that we may always approve ourselves a people mindful of thy favor and glad to do thy will. Bless our land with honorable industry, sound learning, and pure manners. Defend our liberties, preserve our unity. Save us from violence, discord, and confusion; from pride and arrogancy, and from every evil way. Fashion into one happy people the multitude brought hither out of many kindreds and tongues. Endue with the spirit of wisdom those whom we entrust in thy Name with the authority of governance, to the end that there may be peace at home, and that we keep our place among the nations of the earth. In the time of prosperity, temper our self-confidence with thankfulness, and in the day of trouble, suffer not our trust in thee to fail. All which we ask through Jesus Christ our Lord. Amen.   *— George Lyman Locke*

Almighty God, who hast given us this good land for our heritage: We humbly beseech thee that we may always prove ourselves a people mindful of thy favor and glad to do thy will. Bless our land with honorable industry, sound learning, and pure manners. Save us from violence, discord, and confusion; from pride and arrogance, and from every evil way. Defend our liberties, and fashion into one united people the multitudes brought hither out of many kindreds and tongues. Endue with the spirit of wisdom those to whom in thy Name we entrust the authority of government, that there may be justice and peace at home, and that, through obedience to thy law, we may show forth thy praise among the nations of the earth. In the time of prosperity, fill our hearts with thankfulness, and in the day of trouble, suffer not our trust in thee to fail; all which we ask through Jesus Christ our Lord. Amen.
— Book of Common Prayer, 1979

A Thanksgiving for This Land and Prayer for Service

O God, we praise Thee for these blessings, that Thou hast given to us in this land and hast blest it with Thy constant prayer and perfect love. We thank Thee for the gold and the silver and the iron, that we use them for Thy glory for all men's good.

We thank Thee for the mountains, the hills, the lakes, and the rivers. We thank Thee that Thou hast sent the waters out into the valleys to make this world alive in the service of our God.

We thank Thee for everything that Thou hast made. Thou hast made it for the good of men. Morning, noon, and night, we renew our praises.

And now, Father, to use everything for Thy service as Thine own children, for the coming of Thy kingdom, help us this day that we may work with God as children do work with their father, as those do live who live and have their being in Thee; that our corn and our wheat may feed the nations; that our iron may build their ships and carry their food; that our fruit may be for all men; best of all, that our laws, our constitutions, the wisdom Thou hast given the fathers, may live to-day for the blessing and benefit of mankind. Show us, Father, show us where we can work, how we can work, how we can live for God. Bind us together as Thine own children, man with man, state with state, nation with nation, that we all may be one, even as He hath said that we may be one with each other and with our God. We ask it in His name. (The Lord's Prayer follows.)

—*Edward Everett Hale, in the Senate, April 14, 1904*

For the Cooperative Commonwealth

O God, we praise thee for the dream of the golden city of peace and righteousness which has ever haunted the prophets of humanity, and we rejoice with joy unspeakable that at last the people have conquered the freedom and knowledge and power which may avail to turn into reality the vision that so long has beckoned in vain.

Speed now the day when the plains and the hills and the wealth thereof shall be the people's own, and thy freemen shall not live as tenants of men on the earth which thou hast given to all; when no babe shall be born without its equal birthright in the riches and knowledge wrought out by the labor of the ages; and when the mighty engines of industry shall throb with a gladder music because the men who ply these great tools shall be their owners and masters.

Bring to an end, O Lord, the inhumanity of the present, in which all men are ridden by the pale fear of want while the nation of which they are citizens sits throned amid the wealth of their making; when the manhood in some is cowed by helplessness, while the soul of others is surfeited and sick with power which no frail son of the dust should wield.

O God, save us, for our nation is at strife with its own soul and is sinning against the light which thou aforetime hast kindled in it. Thou hast called our people to freedom, but we are withholding from men their share in the common heritage without which freedom becomes a hollow name. Thy Christ has kindled in us the passion for brotherhood, but the social life we have built, denies and slays brotherhood.

We pray thee to revive in us the hardy spirit of our forefathers that we may establish and complete their work, building on the basis of their democracy the firm edifice of a cooperative commonwealth, in which both government and industry shall be of the people, by the people, and for the people. May we, who now live, see the oncoming of the great day of God, when all men shall stand side by side in equal worth and real freedom, all toiling and all reaping, masters of nature but brothers of men, exultant in the tide of the common life, and jubilant in the adoration of Thee, the source of their blessings and the Father of all.

— *Walter Rauschenbusch, 1910*

For the Cooperative Commonwealth
(modern revision)

We praise you, O God, for the dream of the shining city of peace and righteousness which has always haunted the prophets of humanity, and we rejoice with great joy that we have gained freedom and knowledge and power that could enable us to turn into reality the vision that so long has beckoned in vain.

Speed now the day when the wealth of this great land will benefit all who live here, and when no one shall be impoverished by our failure to share the gifts you have given us, when no infant shall be born without its equal birthright in the riches and knowledge won by the labor of the past, and when young people can find the education they need to enrich their lives and the lives of all.

Bring to an end, O God, the inhumanity that leaves so many fearful of their security while others pile up possessions beyond their needs and power beyond what any single person should have.

Save us, O God, for our nation is at war with its own soul and is sinning against the light which you have kindled in it. You have called our people to freedom, but we are withholding from some their share in the common heritage without which freedom becomes a hollow name. Your Christ has kindled in us the passion for equality and friendship, but the social life we have built often denies and slays that vision.

We pray you to revive in us the strong spirit of those who founded this country that we may establish and complete their work, building on the basis of their democracy the firm edifice of a cooperative society in which both government and industry shall be of the people, by the people, and for the people. May we, who now live, see the oncoming of the great day of God, when all people shall stand side by side in equal worth and true freedom, all toiling according to their ability and all reaping according to their need, rejoicing in the sharing of our common life, and jubilant in worshiping you, the source of their blessings and the Creator of all. Amen.

— *Christopher Webber*

A Meditation on Patriotism

Our Father in heaven, make us true lovers of our country; make us true Americans. Help us to keep the promise which our country hath made to the world, to be the home of freedom and justice and brotherhood for all. Enable us in our lives to keep this promise. In our happiness and in our strength put us in mind of the pleasures and the rights of others. Make us brave and truthful and fair. In our play and in our work keep our successes free from boasting and conceit. And when we fail and are defeated, give us a higher courage and a stauncher strength. Help us to become noble and great-hearted citizens, an honour to our nation, and a spring of hope to our neighbors.

— *Henry Sylvester Nash, 1915*

Prayer for the Nation

O God, who by thy providence didst lead our forefathers to this good land wherein they found liberty and freedom to worship Thee: We beseech Thee ever to guide our nation in the way of Thy truth and peace, so that we may never fail in the blessing which Thou hast promised to that people whose God is the Lord; through Jesus Christ Thy Son our Lord. Amen.   — *The Book of Common Worship,*
Presbyterian Church in the United States of America, 1946

O Almighty Lord, who fashionest the hearts of all and considerest all their works; grant, we beseech Thee, to us and to all the people of this land the spirit of obedience to Thy commandments, that walking humbly in Thy fear, we may under Thy mighty protection possess our liberties in righteousness and peace; through Jesus Christ our Lord. *Amen.*

—John Heuss, 1957, adapted

Behold America

Behold, O God, this our beloved country:
>   The old, the young, the little children; rich and poor, ignorant and learned;
>   The laborers and mangers of industry; workers in factory and mine, office and home;
>   A people of many traditions, many colors, divergent hopes and fears.
Behold America:
>   Its mountains and plains, rivers and forests, its inland seas and shining coasts.
Upon this land, upon these people, pour down thy life-giving Spirit of nobility and truth.
>   Where there is strife, bring co-operation for the common good;
>   Where greed and envy abound, control us with that divine perspective which sees in every person the dignity of a growing soul;
>   Where interests clash, set free in us the higher impulse which seeks first thy righteous kingdom, where we may enjoy the glorious liberty of the children of God.

Behold, O Father, this our Nation. Bless it, make it strong
with thy strength, and fill it with the beauty of
holiness; through Jesus Christ our Lord.

— *John Wallace Suter, 1964, adapted*

For Our Country

In the beginning was the Truth, and the Truth was with God,
and the Truth was God. All things were made by him, and
without Truth was not anything made that was made. In the
Truth was life, and that life was the light of all people. The
light of Truth shines in darkness, and the darkness never puts
it out. All who bear witness to Truth bring light to all who
come into the world, that they may believe that Truth finally
prevails.

So we ask the blessing of God upon the searchers for Truth,
and the transmitters of Truth, that they may bring light to the
dark places of the world, to the shadowed side of our nation
and into the dark recesses of our hearts. May the Truth which
alone makes humanity free strengthen the President of the
United States, the Vice-President, and all who have been given
the authority of government to execute justice, to maintain
peace, to bring hope to all humankind.

And may the same light of Truth illumine the hearts of all
the citizens of this land, that honesty, honor, integrity, and
compassion may prevail; and that we all may know in our
personal lives that the important question is never "Will it
work?" but "Is it true?"

So may the moral fiber of this nation be strengthened by
us all — in high estate and low — to show forth the glory of
God in the life of his people, full of grace and truth. Amen.

— *John B. Coburn, 1975, adapted*

A Citizen's Prayer

Let us pay our taxes ... obey the laws of the land ... tell the truth ... obey God rather than man if they are in conflict ... be fearful only of not being true to our true selves ... honor God, through Christ our Lord. Amen.   *—John B. Coburn, 1975*

The Nation

O Lord our Heavenly Father, who dost from Thy throne, behold all the dwellers upon earth; we pray Thee for Thy blessing upon all Christian rulers and magistrates, and more especially upon the President of the United States and the Governor of this State, and upon all these throughout the land who are invested with executive, judicial, or legislative authority. Give them wisdom and grace from above that by their judicious counsel, faithful administration, and good example and influence we may enjoy peace and prosperity, the stability of our Union and of our civil and religious liberties and witness the extension amongst us of sound morals, useful knowledge, and the beneficent arts of social life.

To all bishops and other ministers of Thy Gospel grant Thy spiritual help, that they may faithfully administer Thy sacraments, and teach and preach Thy word to the promotion of pure doctrine and holiness of living amongst Thy people. Endue all teachers of youth in schools and colleges with understanding patience and love, that they may advance the cause of sound learning and godly discipline, and prepare the rising generation to live virtuous, honorable, lives.

And finally, be pleased to suit Thy graces and blessings to our several necessities of soul and body, and dispose us all to glorify Thee in our lives, that after death we may receive the reward of good and faithful servants; through Jesus Christ our Lord. Amen. —*John Heuss, 1957*

Prayer for America

December 12, 1940

Almighty and eternal God, before whom the nations are as the dust of the balance, who hast cast down the mighty from their seat and hast exalted the humble and meek: We bless Thee for all the channels of Thy grace, for joy and pain, freedom and necessity, sunshine and rain, sickness and health; yet most of all we bless Thee for the tender ministries of human love, for the love that binds man and woman, for the unselfishness of parents, for the confidence of little children, and for the encouragement of friends. As Thou hast blessed us, so do Thou quicken within us a deep sense of penitence for the foulness of our cities, the shame of our streets, and the misery of the poor. Let the flood of Thy purifying power cleanse our national life, lest our destruction be determined and we go the way of the nations that have forgotten God. Harken to our prayer, O Lord, for the sake of Thy dear Son, Jesus Christ. Amen. —*Ze Barney Thorne Phillips, 1940–1941*

For the People of Our Land

Father, in the name of Jesus, we come before You to claim Your promise in 2 Chronicles 7:14: "If My people, who are called by My name shall humble themselves, pray, seek, crave, and require of necessity My face and turn from their wicked ways, then will I hear from heaven, forgive their sin, and heal their land."

We are Your people, called by Your name. Thank You for hearing our prayers and moving by Your Spirit in our land. There are famines, earthquakes, floods, natural disasters, and violence occurring. Men's hearts are failing them because of fear.

Lord, Your Son, Jesus, spoke of discerning the signs of the times. With the Holy Spirit as our Helper, we are watching and praying.

We desire to humble ourselves before You, asking that a spirit of humility be released in us. Thank You for quiet and meek spirits, for we know that the meek shall inherit the earth. Search us, O God, and know our hearts; try us, and know our thoughts today. See if there be any wicked way in us, and lead us in the way everlasting.

Forgive us our sins of judging inappropriately, complaining about, and criticizing our leaders. Cleanse us with hyssop, and we will be clean; wash us, and we will be whiter than snow. Touch our lips with coals from Your altar so that we may pray prayers that avail much for all men and women everywhere.

Lord, we desire to release rivers of living water for healing of the nations.

In the name of Jesus, Amen.   — *Germaine Copeland, 1997*

PRAYERS FOR THE GOVERNMENT

The first American colonists came from England, where the Church was established and every service included prayers for the king or queen. In Virginia and colonies where the church was established this custom continued until the American Revolution began. In New England, the Congregational Church was established, and prayers for the state were seldom offered. After the Revolution, Episcopalians substituted

*the name of the President for that of the king and continued
to pray for civil authorities at all services. Other churches
included such prayers or not, depending on their historic relationship with civil authorities, but most often on an optional
and occasional basis. There is, however, a Biblical injunction
to pray for "kings and all who are in high positions" and
prayers for civil authority are becoming more common in all
churches. Perhaps there is, however, a continuing influence of
the days of royalty in the tendency to pray for presidents and
governors and even mayors more often than for the members of the two other co-equal branches of government: the
members of Congress and the Supreme Court.*

For the Government

God, thou great governor of all the world, we pray thee for
all who hold public office and power, for the life, the welfare,
and the virtue of the people are in their hands to make or to
mar. We remember with shame that in the past the mighty
have preyed on the labors of the poor; that they have laid
nations in the dust by their oppression, and have thwarted
the love and the prayers of thy servants. We bless thee that
the new spirit of democracy has touched even yet kings of
the earth. We rejoice that by the free institutions of our country the tyrannous instincts of the strong may be curbed and
turned to the patient service of the commonwealth.

Strengthen the sense of duty in our political life. Grant that
the servants of the state may feel ever more deeply that any
diversion of their public powers for private ends is a betrayal
of their country. Purge our cities and states and nation of
the deep causes of corruption which have so often made sin
profitable and uprightness hard. Bring to an end the stale days
of party cunning. Breathe a new spirit into all our nation.

Lift us from the dust and mire of the past that we may gird ourselves for a new day's work. Give our leaders a new vision of the possible future of our country and set their hearts on fire with large resolves. Raise up a new generation of public men, who will have the faith and daring of the Kingdom of God in their hearts, and who will enlist for life in a holy warfare for the freedom and rights of the people.

— *Walter Rauschenbusch, 1910*

For the Nation and Its Government

Almighty God, may Thy loving-kindness be upon us and establish Thou the works of our hands, yea, the work of our hands, firmly establish Thou it. We pray Thee to look down in Thy infinite kindness upon the Members of this House; be graciously inclined toward them and endow them with a good heart, with wisdom and understanding, and with a just and willing mind, so that they may acquit themselves of and discharge their duties as fully as their hearts desire to do so.

We thank Thee, O God, for the preservation of this great and glorious Republic, in its national integrity and unity, and humbly do we pray Thee for strength and courage that we may purge wherever it exists our citizen States of the deep causes of corruption which so often make sin profitable and uprightness hard. Do Thou grant unto our public men the faith and daring of the kingdom of God in their hearts so that they may enlist in the sacred warfare for the freedom and the rights of the people.

Into Thy keeping, O Father, do we commend the President of these United States and Members of this House and all the constituted authorities, so that through them order may be preserved and right and liberty be fostered. Do Thou strengthen the bonds of loyalty and friendship between all the inhabitants of our great country. Bless all mankind, Thy children, now and forever-more. Amen.

— *Isidore Lewinthal, in the United States Senate, July 1, 1912*

A Prayer for Good Government

O God, whose blessed Son wept over the sins of Jerusalem; Grant to us searchings of heart because of the sins of this community; vouchsafe to us such officers as shall, without fear or favour, boldly maintain the law; so that truth and morality, religion and honour may be established among us for ever; through Jesus Christ our Lord. Amen.

— *Charles Lewis Slattery, 1922*

For the President of the United States and All in Civil Authority

O Lord our Governor, whose glory is in all the world: We commend this nation to your merciful care, that, being guided by thy Providence, we may dwell secure in your peace. Grant to the President of the United States, the Governor of this State (*or* Commonwealth), and to all in authority, wisdom and strength to know and to do your will. Fill them with the love of truth and righteousness, and make them ever mindful of their calling to serve this people in your fear; through Jesus Christ our Lord, who lives and reigns with you and the Holy Spirit, one God, world without end. Amen.

— *Book of Common Prayer, 1979*

For the Head of Government

Gracious and sovereign Lord, we pray for Your servant, the head of our government, that You might keep him faithful to the solemn office with which You have charged him. Strengthen him and uphold him. Guide and direct him to fulfill Your purposes. Give him counsel and aid that he may preserve the integrity and honor of our nation. Give him firmness to maintain law and justice, and determination to strive for peace with all nations. Give him wisdom in the hours of decision. Give him serenity in the face of crises. Give him courage in the moments of danger. Protect him from assassins and ill health. Guard and defend him that he may serve the security and well-being of his people. Make him a leader of a people who will do Your righteous and holy will among the nations of the earth. We ask it in the name of Your most holy Son, our Lord. Amen.

— The Lutheran Book of Prayer, 1970

For the Congress

A Prayer for Congress.
To be used during their Session.

Gracious God, we humbly beseech thee, as for the people of these United States in general, so especially for their Senate and Representatives in Congress assembled; that thou wouldest be pleased to direct and prosper all their consultations, to the advancement of thy glory, the good of thy Church, the safety, honour, and welfare of thy people; that all things may be so ordered and settled by their endeavours, upon the best and surest foundations, that peace and happiness, truth and justice, religion and piety, may be established among us for all generations. These and all other necessaries for them, for us, and thy whole Church, we humbly beg in the Name and mediation of Jesus Christ, our most blessed Lord and Saviour. Amen.   *— Book of Common Prayer, 1928*

A Prayer for the Congress

The following prayer was the first to be offered by a Muslim in the United States Congress.

In the name of God, most gracious, most merciful:
  Praise belongs to Thee alone, Oh God, Lord, and Creator
      of all the world;
  Praise belongs to Thee who shaped us and colored us in
      the wombs of our mothers; colored us black and
      white, brown, red, and yellow;
  Praise belongs to Thee, who created us from males and
      females and made us into nations and tribes that we
      may know each other;
  Most gracious, most merciful, all knowing, all wise, just
      God;
  Master of the day of judgment, Thee alone do we worship
      and from Thee alone do we seek help;
  Guide the leaders of this Nation, who have been given a
      great responsibility in worldly affairs, guide them
      and grant them righteousness and wisdom;
  Guide them and us on the straight path, the path of those
      [on] whom Thou hast bestowed Thy favors, the
      path of your inspired servants, the path of Abraham,
      Moses, Jesus, and Muhammad;
  Guide them and us not on the path of the disobedient ones
      who have earned Your wrath and displeasure. Amen
                                    — *Siraj Wahaj, June 25, 1991*

The Supreme Court

O God of truth and justice, who art a discerner of the thoughts and intents of the heart, and before whose throne all must stand to be judged: Give we pray thee, to the members of the

Supreme Court of the United States, wisdom and understanding to judge aright; that discerning between good and evil, they may help our nation to move in harmony with thy purpose for all mankind; through Jesus Christ our Lord. Amen.

—John Wallace Suter, 1964

For Systems of Justice

Lord Jesus,

> You were in prison, found guilty when you were innocent;
> You were executed as traitor when in fact you were Savior,

To you who died to set all people free we pray for:

> All makers of the laws of the land, that they do so with reason and compassion.
>
> All interpreters of the law — judges, lawyers — that they be fair, honest, and impartial.
>
> All administrators of the law — prison guards and superintendents — that they be merciful in their firmness.
>
> All prisoners — that they may know that you are in prison with them, to their homes with their loved ones, and that to you is their hope. Though bound, may they be perfectly free to you and to your service.

We pray also for the systems that make for peace in a divided world — journeys of people of goodwill who meet on neutral ground to bring an end to warfare and destruction. The cry of anguish of prisoners and innocent sufferers, of their families, is your cry, Lord Jesus — and we utter it with you.

So also may the nations united for peace be made strong. Prosper those who serve the cause of the United Nations, that together all nations may walk to the ways of peace and establish an ordered world of justice and decency for all.

—John B. Coburn, 1975, adapted

A Prayer for the Courts of Justice

O Almighty and everlasting God, we make our humble supplication to thy Divine Majesty, humbly imploring thy protection and blessing to the People and Government of the United States of America, and especially on the People and Government of this State in which we live; Entreating thy favour and gracious Goodness towards them: Particularly we make our prayers to thee in behalf of this Court, by thy good Providence, now assembled for the administration of Justice to thy People.

Look with favour, O God, on the Judges of the Court — on the subordinate Officers belonging to it — and on all concerned in the administration of justice in it. Direct them by thy Grace in whatever business shall come before them; and grant that all their decisions may be grounded on the principles of Truth and Equity, so that Peace and Happiness, Justice and Righteousness, Religion and Piety may flourish among us for all generations: and, that thy People being secure, through the protection of equal Law, and the administration of equal justice, may joyfully serve thee in all Godly quietness; — may live in peace with each other and in peace and friendship with all mankind. Hear us, we beseech thee, O God, for the sake of Jesus Christ, our Redeemer and Saviour.

— Samuel Seabury, c. 1786

For Officers of the Law

Heavenly Father, we commend to Your care those who enforce law among us. Watch over them. Protect them from harm and danger. Keep them from the temptations to apply force improperly, to use their authority unwisely, to rely on the instruments of coercion exclusively, to yield to bribery or dishonesty. Keep them from rancor or hatred towards those whom they must apprehend.

Equip them with the ability to detect the sources of crime and violence. Give them courage when they are in danger. Give them strength as our defenders. Give them gentleness when they serve those who are hurt or neglected. Give them faithfulness to their task. Give them sympathy for those whom they serve. Reward them with the joys of rendering service that conforms to your most holy will. We pray in Jesus' name. Amen.   — *The Lutheran Book of Prayer, 1970*

IN TIMES OF WAR OR CRISIS

In Time of War

Sovereign Lord, deal with us according to Your mercy. Forgive humankind for its inability to rise above the wrath and fury of war. Comfort all who mourn the losses of dear ones, who are homeless, and who are displaced by the violence of war. Prepare for death those who give themselves in sacrificial service. Stir your people to valor and honor, but keep them humble and contrite. Raise up leaders who are able to bring peace out of our confusions. Restore order and justice where chaos and corruption must be overcome. Keep this war within the bounds of controllable limits. Hold us back from the futility of unleashing the full potential of nuclear war.

Above all, bring to a swift close this conflict. Cause the nations to resolve their differences by a mutual desire for equity. Hasten the day when all may return to useful tasks. If warfare continues, give us the vision to see Your will and to move swiftly to accomplish the same; through Christ, our Lord. Amen.   — *The Lutheran Book of Prayer, 1970, adapted*

During a National Crisis

> God of ages,
> In your sight nations rise and fall,
> and pass through times of peril.
> Now when our land is troubled,
> be near to judge and save.
> May leaders be led by your wisdom;
> may they search your will and see it clearly.
> If we have turned from your way,
> help us to reverse our ways and repent.
> Give us your light and your truth to guide us;
> through Jesus Christ
> who is Lord of this world, and our Savior. Amen.
>   — *The Book of Common Worship,*
>   *Presbyterian Church in the*
>   *United States of America, 1946*

PRAYERS FOR NATIONAL FORGIVENESS AND RENEWAL

A Prayer for Forgiveness

We beseech Thee, O God, to forgive those national sins which do so easily beset us: our wanton waste of the wealth of soil and sea; our desecration of natural beauty; our heedlessness of those who come after us, if only we be served; our love of money, our contempt for small things and our worship of big things; our neglect of backward peoples; our complacency; and our pride of life. For these wrongs done to our land and our heritage, as for right things left undone, forgive us, O Lord. Amen.

> — *The Book of Common Worship, Presbyterian Church*
> *in the United States of America, 1946*

Prayer of Confession

God our Father: you led us to this land, and, out of conflict, created in us a love of peace and liberty. We have failed you by neglecting rights and restricting freedoms. Forgive pride that overlooks national wrong, or justifies injustice. Forgive divisions caused by prejudice or greed. Have mercy, God, on the heart of this land. Make us compassionate, fair, and helpful to each other. Raise up in us a right patriotism, that sees and seeks this nation's good; through Jesus Christ the Lord. Amen. — *The Worshipbook, 1975*

A Prayer for Forgiveness

Almighty God, ruler of all the peoples of the earth,
forgive, we pray, our shortcomings;
purify our hearts to see and love truth;
give wisdom to our counselors
and steadfastness to our people;
and bring us at last to the fair city of peace,
whose foundations are mercy, justice, and good will,
and whose builder and maker you are;
through your son, Jesus Christ our Lord. Amen.
— *Woodrow Wilson, 1856–1924,*
The Book of Common Worship, Presbyterian Church
in the United States of America, 1993

America Confesses

Our Father, bring to the remembrance of Thy people Thine ancient and time-honored promise: "If my people, which are called by my name, shall humble themselves, and pray, and seek my face, and turn from their wicked ways; then will I hear from heaven, and will forgive their sin, and will heal their land."

We — this company of Thy people assembled — would begin now to meet the conditions that will enable Thee to fulfill Thy promise.

May all of America come to understand that right-living alone exalteth a nation, that only in Thy will can peace and joy be found. But, Lord, this land cannot be righteous unless her people are righteous, and we, here gathered, are part of America. We know that the world cannot be changed until the hearts of men are changed. Our hearts need to be changed.

We therefore confess to Thee that:

Wrong ideas and sinful living have cut us off from Thee.
We have been greedy.
We have sought to hide behind barricades of selfishness;
    shackles have imprisoned the great heart of America.
We have tried to isolate ourselves from the bleeding
    wounds of a blundering world.
In our self-sufficiency we have sought not Thy help.
We have held conferences and ignored Thee completely.
We have disguised selfishness as patriotism; our arrogance
        has masqueraded as pride.
We have frittered away time and opportunities while the
        world bled.
Our ambitions have blinded us to opportunities.
We have bickered in factory and business, and sought
    to solve our differences only through self-interest.

Lord God of Hosts, forgive us, O God, by Thy guidance and Thy power may our beloved land once again become God's own country, a nation contrite in heart, confessing her sins; a nation keenly sensitive to all the unresolved injustice and wrong still in our midst.

Hear this our prayer and grant that we may confidently expect to see it answered in our time, through Jesus Christ, our Lord. Amen. — *Peter Marshall, 1949*

FOR JUSTICE

God's Justice Be Done on Earth

O Lord, Love incarnate,
    for this You have come among us
    to set the captive free,
    to give sight to the blind,
    to free the oppressed,
    to proclaim the good news to the poor.
Help us follow the footsteps of Christ
    and live out Your love.

May Your Kingdom of justice come.

O Lord, You who search the human heart,
    You are concerned with our world,
    attentive to every act of injustice, suffering,
    oppression and deceit.
May the Holy Spirit enlighten our hearts
    that we may rebuke ourselves on account of sin,
    righteousness and judgment,
    and turn back to You.

May Your Kingdom of justice come.

Now we whom You have freed
    cry out to You with one voice:
Help us who have received mercy to be merciful
    to those who are oppressed and wronged

and we ask that according to Your mercy and grace,
they may receive Your compassion.

May Your Kingdom of justice come.

O Lord, Your love and mercy
   have been revealed on earth;
For the sake of Christ and all those
   who truly follow Him.
      With justice and righteousness,
You will establish the kingdom.

**May Your justice and praise
   spring up before all nations,
   for the zeal of the Lord God will accomplish it.**

Amen.

Yes, Jesus,
I want to be on Your right side or Your left side,
   not for any selfish reason.
I want to be on Your right or Your best side,
   not in terms of some political kingdom or ambition
but I just want to be there
   in love and in justice and in truth
   and in commitment to others,
   so we can make of this old world a new world,

Amen.   — *Martin Luther King Jr.*

FOR PEACE

Against War

Lord, since first the blood of Abel cried to thee from the ground that drank it, this earth of thine has been defiled with the blood of man shed by his brother's hand, and the centuries sob with the ceaseless horror of war. Ever the pride of kings and the covetousness of the strong has driven peaceful nations to slaughter. Ever the songs of the past and the pomp of armies have been used to inflame the passions of the people. Our spirit cries out to thee in revolt against it, and we know that our righteous anger is answered by thy holy wrath.

Break thou the spell of the enchantments that make the nations drunk with the lust of battle and draw them on as willing tools of death. Grant us a quiet and steadfast mind when our own nation clamors for vengeance or aggression. Strengthen our sense of justice and our regard for the equal worth of other peoples and races. Grant to the rulers of nations faith in the possibility of peace through justice, and grant to the common people a new and stern enthusiasm for the cause of peace. Bless our soldiers and sailors for their swift obedience and their willingness to answer to the call of duty, but inspire them none the less with a hatred of war, and may they never for love of private glory or advancement provoke its coming. May our young men still rejoice to die for their country with the valor of their fathers, but teach our age nobler methods of matching our strength and more effective ways of giving our life for the flag.

O thou strong Father of all nations, draw all thy great family together with an increasing sense of our common blood and destiny, that peace may come on earth at last, and thy sun may shed its light rejoicing on a holy brotherhood of peoples.

— *Walter Rauschenbusch, 1910*

For Peace

Almighty God, Ruler of all things and all people:
  You hold the universe in Your palm,
  You have set all things to move in harmony,
  You desire that we dwell in unity and love.
We confess
  we have spoiled creation by our sin,
  we have disrupted harmony by our rebellion,
  we have divided our nation by selfishness.
We trust
  You will not permit sin to rule the day,
  You can bring order out of our confusion,
  You make nations instruments of Your will.
We implore You that You would
  crush our lust for illicit power,
  stir in us respect for Your creation,
  kindle in us love for Your creatures.
To this end, we pray:
  raise up leaders everywhere who do Your will,
  make the nations obedient servants of Your purpose,
  teach us to live in service to one another.
Grant tranquillity, that the peace which the world cannot
      understand
  may be preached to the nations in the name of Your Son
      Jesus. Amen.
                    — *The Lutheran Book of Prayer, 1970, adapted*

For World Peace

O thou almighty God, who alone canst bring peace and salvation to our troubled world, hasten the day when all people
shall acknowledge thee as Lord.

Quell, we beseech thee, the suspicious cries of nation against nation. Rid us of the shackles of sectionalism, racial tension, national arrogance, and disentangle us from our corporate and individual selfishness. Arouse in us a genuine belief in our brotherhood so that in the spirit of mutual helpfulness the strong may use their power not to divide and conquer, but to unite and enrich the weak. Beat the dreadful implements of war into the creative tools of peace. Bind together the people of the East and West, North and South, by ties of sympathy, respect, and service, and raise up leaders of vision and courage. Establish thy grace, dear Lord, in each of our hearts throughout the world that we may appreciate each other's virtues, patiently forbear each other's differences and so become unified into one family, living to glorify thee.

— *The New Worship Handbook*
(adapted from Bishop Charles Henry Brent)

For World Peace

The concern which I lay before God today is:
>my concern for the life of the world in these troubled
>>times.
>I confess my own inner confusion as I look out upon the
>>world.
>>There is food for all — many are hungry.
>>There are clothes enough for all — many are in rags.
>>There is room enough for all — many are crowded.
>>There are none who want war — preparations for war
>>>abound.
>I confess my own share in the ills of the times.
>>I have shirked my own responsibility as a citizen,
>>I have not been wise in casting my ballot.

I have left to others a real interest in making a public
   opinion worthy of democracy.
I have been concerned about my own little job, my own
   little security, my own shelter, my own bread.
I have not really cared about jobs for others, security
   for others, bread for others,
I have not worked for peace; I want peace, but I have
   voted and worked for war.
I have silenced my own voice that it may not be heard
   on the side of any causes, however right,
      if it meant running risks or damaging my own little
      reputation.
Let thy light burn in me that I may, from this moment on,
   take effective steps within my own powers,
      to live up to the light and courageously to pay for
      the kind of world I do deeply desire.

Our Father, fresh from the world, with the smell of life upon
us, we make an act of prayer in the silence of this place.
Our minds are troubled because the anxieties of our hearts
are deep and searching. We are stifled by the odor of death
which envelops our earth, where in so many places brother
fights against brother. The panic of fear, the torture of insecurity, the ache of hunger, all have fed and rekindled ancient
hatreds and long-forgotten memories of old struggles, when
the world was young and Thy children were but dimly aware
of Thy Presence in the midst. For all this, we seek forgiveness. There is no one of us without guilt and, before Thee,
we confess our sins: we are proud and arrogant; we are selfish
and greedy; we have hatred in our hearts and minds, much
that makes for bitterness, hatred, and revenge. While we wait
in Thy Presence, search our Spirits and grant to our minds
the guidance and the wisdom that will teach us the way to

take, without which there can be no peace and no confidence anywhere. Teach us how to put at the disposal of Thy Purposes of Peace the fruits of our industry, the products of our minds, the vast wealth of our land and the resources of our spirit. Grant unto us the courage to follow the illumination of this hour to the end that we shall not lead death to anyone's door; but rather may we strengthen the hands of all in high places, and in common tasks seek to build a friendly world, of friendly people, beneath a friendly sky. This is the simple desire of our hearts which we share with Thee in thanksgiving and confidence. — *Howard Thurman, 1976, adapted*

Muslim Prayer for Peace

In the name of Allah,
the beneficent, the merciful.
Praise be to the Lord of the Universe
who has created us
and made us into tribes and nations
that we may know each other,
not that we may despise each other.
If the enemy incline towards peace,
do thou also incline towards peace,
and trust God,
for the Lord is the one
that heareth and knoweth all things.
And the servants of God,
most gracious are those
who walk on the Earth in humility.
— *Islamic Society*
of North America, 2007

NATIONAL THANKSGIVINGS

Prayer of Thanksgiving

Great God: we thank you for this land so fair and free; for its worthy aims and charities. We are grateful for people who have come to our shores, with customs and accents to enrich our lives. You have led us in the past, forgiven evil, and will lead us in time to come. Give us a voice to praise your goodness in this land, and a will to serve you, now and always; through Jesus Christ our Lord. Amen.

— The Worshipbook, 1975, adapted

LITANIES

The Litany is one of the oldest forms of Christian prayer and is ideally suited to the involvement of the congregation in the offering of prayer. The traditions that came to this country had largely lost that sense of congregational involvement and centered either on a priest at the altar or a preacher in the pulpit. The ease with which printed orders of service can now be produced makes the Litany form easier to use and most churches now make common use of both ancient and modern litanies.

A Native American Thanksgiving for the Americas and Their People

This Litany was used at a service commemorating the 500th anniversary of the landing in the Western Hemisphere of Christopher Columbus. The service was held at the National Cathedral in Washington on October 12, 1992.

Leader: For our ancestors who built nations and cultures; who thrived and prospered long before the coming of strangers; for the forfeit of their lives, their homes, their lands, and their freedoms sacrificed to the rise of new nations and new worlds.

All: *We offer a song of honor and thanks.*

Leader: For the wealth of our lands; for minerals in the earth; for the plants and waters and animals on the earth; for the birds, the clouds and rain; for the sun and moon in the sky and the gifts they gave to our people that enabled the rise of new world economies.

All: *We offer a song of honor and thanks.*

Leader: For the many foods coaxed from the heart of Mother Earth; for the skills we were given to develop foods that now belong to the world: potatoes, corn, beans, squash, peanuts, tomatoes, peppers, coffee, cocoa, sugar, and many, many more.

All: *We offer a song of honor and thanks.*

Leader: For the medicines first discovered by our ancestors and now known to the world: quinine, ipecac, iodine, curare, petroleum jelly, witch hazel, and others; for the healing skills of our people and those who now care for us. For tobacco, sage, sweet grass, and cedar that give spiritual healing by the power of their meaning.

All: *We offer a song of honor and thanks.*

Leader: For oceans, streams, rivers, lakes, and other waters of our lands that provide bountifully for us; for clams, lobsters, salmon, trout, shrimp, and abalone; for the pathways the waters have provided.

All: *We offer a song of honor and thanks.*

Leader: For the friendship that first welcomed all to our
          shores; for the courage of those who watched their
          worlds change and disappear and for those who led
          in the search for new lives; for our leaders today who
          fight with courage and great heart for us.

All: *We offer a song of honor and thanks.*

Leader: For the friends who suffered with us and stand with
          us today to help bring the promise and the hope that
          the New World meant to their ancestors.

All: *We offer a song of honor and thanks.*

Leader: For the strength and beauty of our diverse Native
          cultures; for the traditions that give structure to our
          lives, that define who we are; for the skills of our
          artists and crafts people and the gifts of their hands.

All: *We offer a song of honor and thanks.*

Leader: For the spirituality and vision that gave our people
          the courage and faith to endure; that brought many
          to an understanding and acceptance of the love of
          Christ, our Brother and Savior.

All: *We offer a song of honor and thanks.*

Leader: Accept, O God, Creator, our honor song, and make
          our hearts thankful for what we have been given.
          Make us humble for what we have taken. Make us
          glad as we return some measure of what we have
          been given. Strengthen our faith and make us strong
          in the service of our people, in the name of our
          Brother and Savior, Jesus Christ, your Son, in the
          power of the Holy Spirit. Amen.

                                    — *The Wideness of God's Mercy,* 2007

Litany for the Nation

This litany is designed to be used on days of national celebration, or in times of national crisis.

Leader: Mighty God: the earth is yours and nations are your people. Take away our pride and bring to mind your goodness, so that, living together in this land, we may enjoy your gifts and be thankful.

People: *Amen.*

Leader: For clouded mountains, fields and woodland; for shoreline and running streams; for all that makes our nation good and lovely;

People: *We thank you, God.*

Leader: For farms and villages where food is gathered to feed our people;

People: *We thank you, God.*

Leader: For cities where people talk and work together in factories, shops, or schools to shape those things we need for living;

People: *We thank you, God.*

Leader: For explorers, planners, statesmen; for prophets who speak out, and for silent faithful people; for all who love our land and guard freedom;

People: *We thank you, God.*

Leader: For vision to see your purpose hidden in our nation's history, and courage to seek it in human love exchanged;

People: *We thank you, God.*

Leader: O God: your justice is like rock, and your mercy like pure flowing water. Judge and forgive us. If we have turned from you, return us to your way; for without you we are lost people. From brassy patriotism and a blind trust in power;

People: *Deliver us, O God.*

Leader: From public deceptions that weaken trust; from self-seeking in high political places;

People: *Deliver us, O God.*

Leader: From divisions among us of class or race; from wealth that will not share, and poverty that feeds on food of bitterness;

People: *Deliver us, O God.*

Leader: From neglecting rights; from overlooking the hurt, the imprisoned, and the needy among us;

People: *Deliver us, O God.*

Leader: From a lack of concern for other lands and peoples; from narrowness of national purpose; from failure to welcome the peace you promise on earth;

People: *Deliver us, O God.*

Leader: Eternal God: before you nations rise and fall; they grow strong or wither by your design. Help us to repent our country's wrong, and to choose your right in reunion and renewal.

People: *Amen.*

Leader: Give us a glimpse of the Holy City you are bringing to earth, where death and pain and crying will be gone away; and nations gather in the light of your presence.

People: *Great God, renew this nation.*

Leader: Teach us peace, so that we may plow up battlefields and pound weapons into building tools, and learn to talk across old boundaries as brothers and sisters in your love.

People: *Great God, renew this nation.*

Leader: Talk sense to us, so that we may wisely end all prejudice, and may put a stop to cruelty, which divides or wounds the human family.

People: *Great God, renew this nation.*

Leader: Draw us together as one people who do your will, so that our land may be a light to nations, leading the way to your promised kingdom, which is coming among us.

People: *Great God, renew this nation.*

Leader: Great God, eternal Lord: long years ago you gave our fathers this land as a home for the free. Show us there is no law or liberty apart from you; and let us serve you modestly, as devoted people; through Jesus Christ our Lord.

People: *Amen.*   — *The Worshipbook, 1975, adapted*

Litany for the Nation

Almighty God, ruler of nations, to whose grace we owe the manifold blessings of this land,

We worship you with grateful hearts.

We confess that in many ways we have turned aside from your commandments, and it is because of your steadfast love that we are not consumed. You offer us mercy and forgiveness, though we have rebelled against you, and have not obeyed your command to walk in your laws, which you have set before us.

Lord, have mercy on us, and blot out our transgressions.

We pray, Lord, that you will guide and bless all who are in places of authority. Protect them from violence, and fill the hearts of the people with respect and love for them, because you have established their authority. Raise up for us leaders who will carry out all your purpose, and, in patience and courage, will depend on you.

Save your people, and bless your heritage.

Make of this nation an instrument for the promotion of peace, freedom, and righteousness. May it be a haven for the oppressed of other lands, a home of happiness for all who dwell within its borders; and may our commitment to liberty and justice for all be preserved for the generations to come.

Hear us, gracious Lord and God.

Guide us and our leaders through the Spirit of Christ's love as we struggle with matters of teaching and learning, home and family, health and security, work and justice. Turn the hearts of all people to you, that they may seek eternal life through Jesus Christ, who redeems us and our world.

Hear us, gracious Lord and God.

Grant wisdom to those who are of the family of faith. Enable us to accept the authority of government for your sake, ready for every good work, abstaining from every form of evil, and paying to all whatever is due them. As citizens of this nation may we bring credit to our Savior in all we do.

Hear us, gracious Lord and God.

Grant to the people of this and all other lands a love of peace and order that the nations shall learn war no more. Hasten the day when the kingdom of the world shall become the Kingdom of our Lord and of his Christ, and he will reign forever and ever.

Hear us, gracious Lord and God. Amen
— *The Moravian Book of Worship, 1995*

For the Nation and Peace

Leader: Eternal God, who brought forth all worlds from the womb of your being and nurtured creation to splendor in the cradle of your care:

People: *We praise you for your loving-kindness toward all you have made and for a universe still expanding beyond the stars.*

Leader: We rejoice that you have raised us from dust and breathed living breath into our frames, that we may love and serve you in perfect freedom.

People: *We lift before you a world burdened with the power to incinerate itself and to return to you the breathless dust of a silenced earth.*

Leader: God, in your mercy, show us the way of justice and peace, lest in the defense of what cannot be defended, we offer death a winnerless victory.

People: *Speak to all peoples, but speak especially to us, that
         our nation may not lift up sword against any nation,
         neither provoke war by a readiness that invites war.*

Leader: God, in your gentleness, wean us from the enemy
         within ourselves, that we may have grace and courage
         to prepare for peace with more diligence than any
         who labor to prepare for war.

People: *Forgive us for not doing anything, because we can-
         not do everything, and for not taking first steps,
         because we cannot see the last step on the journey
         that peace requires.*

Leader: God, in your faithfulness, do not turn away from us
         when we place our trust in megatons of destruction
         rather than in you.

People: *From the lips of Jesus Christ, let us hear again the
         call, "Blessed are those who work for peace; they
         shall be called the children of God."*

Leader: Come, Holy Spirit, let your tongues of fire stir us to a
         Pentecost of peace, lest the tongues of the technicians
         of war vaporize us in a holocaust of hate.

People: *Hear our prayer, O God, for the sake of the world
         you pronounced good at the dawn of creation, and
         for the world you loved enough to send us Jesus
         Christ, who with you and the Holy Spirit lives and
         reigns, one God, for ever and ever. Amen.*
         — *Book of Worship, United Church of Christ, 1986*

In Thanksgiving for Our Country

O eternal God, ruler of all the earth, we bless you for our
country. Bountifully have you given to us, beyond all our

deserving. You have made us heirs of what the untold ages have created: the majesty of upthrust mountains, the green of wooded hills, the prairies rolling to their far horizons, the fertile valleys where the rivers run. All that we can accomplish rests on this which you have freely given. Hear us as we bring you the tribute of our grateful hearts.

For all the mighty width of land from bordering sea to sea,

We thank you, O Lord.

For endless fields where the grain harvests ripen, for orchards with their golden fruit,

We thank you, O Lord.

For cattle in the meadows, for wildlife in the woods, for the fish in the ocean and lakes and mountain streams, for the homely creatures of the farm, and for the infinite beauty of winged birds,

We thank you, O Lord.

For rich ores hidden in the hills, for coal and oil and iron, and for all the treasures of unnumbered mines,

We thank you, O Lord.

For the strength and skill of all the toiling multitude on whom our life depends: on farms, in fishing fleets, in factories, and before the fires of furnaces and mills,

We thank you, O Lord.

For the genius of inventors, for the imagination of engineers, for the daring of those who have dreamed a mightier civilization and have fashioned their dreams in stone and steel,

We thank you, O Lord.

For those who laid the railroads and launched the ships, for those who have built the bridges and lifted the towers of cities to the sky,

We thank you, O Lord.

For all the host of men and women who in industry, in commerce, and in communications hold the world together because they are dependable at their daily posts,

We thank you, O Lord.

For all the servants of the mind, for scholars and teachers, for authors and artists, and for all poets in word or deed who reveal the wideness and wonder of the world,

We thank you, O Lord.

Yet we remember that as we have greatly received, so in the same measure we are responsible. Forbid that we should betray our trust, or that the fire which has been passed on to us should perish. Help us to be worthy of our forebears, and of their God. To all the high desires of the pioneers and prophets,

O God, help us to be faithful.

To their belief in the possibilities of the common people,

O God, help us to be faithful.

To their passion for freedom and their readiness to live and die in its defense,

O God, help us to be faithful.

To their scorn of tyranny, and their trust in ordinary folk to rule themselves,

O God, help us to be faithful.

To their vision of a human commonwealth in which people from many lands might share,

O God, help us to be faithful.

To their release from the prejudices and passions of an old world and their will to build a new,

O God, help us to be faithful.

O God, our mothers and fathers trusted in you

And were not confounded.

They lifted their faces to you

And were not ashamed.

So enlighten us, O Father, and lead us on your redeeming way; through Jesus Christ our Lord. Amen.

— *Walter Russell Bowie, 1956*

PART TWO

Prayers from American History

THE NEW NATION

*When the suggestion was made that the first session of the
Continental Congress be opened with prayer, two delegates
objected on the grounds that the members were so divided
among various churches that "we could not join in the same
act of worship." Samuel Adams then responded that he was
not a bigot and "could hear a prayer from a gentleman of
piety and virtue who was at the same time a friend to his
country." He added that he had heard of an Episcopal clergyman named Jacob Duché who had such a character and
therefore moved that he be invited to offer prayers at the first
session. This motion was seconded and passed, and the next
morning Mr. Duché appeared, read Psalm 95, and offered the
following prayer extemporaneously.*

The First Prayer in Congress, September 7, 1774

O Lord our Heavenly Father, high and mighty King of kings,
and Lord of lords, who dost from thy throne behold all the
dwellers on earth and reignest with power supreme and un-
contolled over all the Kingdoms, Empires and Governments;
look down in mercy, we beseech thee, on these our American
States, who have fled to thee from the rod of the oppressor
and thrown themselves on Thy gracious protection, desiring
to be henceforth dependent only on Thee, to Thee have they
appealed for the righteousness of their cause; to Thee do they
now look up for that countenance and support, which Thou
alone canst give; take them, therefore, Heavenly Father, under
Thy nurturing care; give them wisdom in Council and valor
in the field; defeat the malicious designs of our cruel adversaries; convince them of the unrighteousness of their Cause

and if they persist in their sanguinary purposes, O! Let the voice of Thy unerring justice, sounding in their hearts, constrain them to drop the weapons of war from their unnerved hands in the day of battle!

Be Thou present, O God of wisdom, and direct the councils of this honorable assembly; enable them to settle things on the best and surest foundation. That the scene of blood may be speedily closed; that order, harmony and peace may be effectually restored, and truth and justice, religion and piety, prevail and flourish amongst the people. Preserve the health of their bodies and vigor of their minds; shower down on them and the millions they here represent, such temporal blessings as Thou seest expedient for them in this world and crown them with everlasting glory in the world to come. All this we ask In the name and through the merits of Jesus Christ, Thy Son and our Savior. Amen.   — *Jacob Duché, 1774*

THE AMERICAN REVOLUTION

The American Revolution has often been described as a "Civil War" since many of the colonists sided with the British government. Some fled to Canada while others remained and prayed for the restoration of peace and unity. The following form was provided for the use of those seeking peace and a restoration of British rule. It is a useful reminder that prayers are often offered at cross purposes and that some words like "nevertheless not my will but thine be done" should always be added to our prayers either aloud or silently.

O Almighty God, who rulest over all the kingdoms of the earth, and on whose most gracious providence they depend evermore for preservation and prosperity; Extend thine accustomed goodness to the people of this land; who looking up to thee as the supreme author of all blessings, and the sure safeguard and mighty deliverer in all dangers and difficulties, do now implore thy watchful care and protection, beseeching thee to guide them continually with thy counsel, to strengthen them with thy powerful arm, and to crown with success their necessary endeavours in defeating the unjust attempts of their rebellious fellow-subjects against the rights of our Sovereign, and the lawful authority of the legislature of these kingdoms. Grant this, O merciful Father, for Jesus Christ's sake, our only Lord and Saviour. Amen.

O Lord God of our salvation, in whose hands are the issues of life and death, of good and evil, and without whose aid the wisest counsels of frail men, and the multitude of an host, and all the instruments of war are but weak and vain; incline thine ear, we pray thee, to the earnest and devout supplications of thy servants, who, not confiding in the splendour of any thing that is great, or the stability of any thing that is strong here below, do most humbly flee, O Lord, unto thee for succour, and put their trust under the shadow of thy wings. Be thou to us a tower of defence against the assaults of our enemies, our shield and buckler in the day of battle and so bless the arms of our gracious Sovereign, in the maintenance of His just and lawful rights, and prosper His endeavours to restore tranquillity among His unhappy deluded subjects in *America*, now in open rebellion against His Crown, in defiance of all subordination and legal government, that we being preserved by thy help and goodness from all perils and disasters, and made happily triumphant over all the disturbers of our peace, may joyfully laud and magnify thy glorious Name and serve thee from generation to generation in all godliness and quietness, through Jesus Christ our Lord. Amen.

A Prayer for Unity

O God, who hast taught us in thy holy Word, to increase and abound in love one towards another, put away from us, we beseech thee, all bitterness and wrath, and evil-speaking and envy, that our hearts may be firmly knit together in mutual affection, in zeal for our religion and laws, in dutiful obedience to the King, and all who are in authority under him, that as there is but one body and one Spirit, and one hope of our calling, one faith, one God and Father of us all, we may henceforth be all of one heart and of one soul, united in one holy bond of truth and peace, and may with one mind and one mouth glorify thee, O God, through Jesus Christ our Lord. Amen.

A Prayer for Our Enemies

O Blessed Lord, who hast commanded us by thy beloved Son to love our Enemies, and to extend our charity in praying even for those, who despitefully use us, give grace, we beseech thee, to our unhappy fellow subjects in *America*, that seeing and confessing the error of their ways, and having a due sense of their ingratitude for the many blessings of thy Providence, preserved to them by the indulgent care and protection of these kingdoms, they may again return to their duty, and make themselves worthy of thy pardon and forgiveness: Grant us in the mean time not only strength and courage to withstand them, but charity to forgive and pity them, to shew a willingness to receive them again as friends and brethren, upon just and reasonable terms, and to treat them with mercy and kindness, for the sake of thy Son Jesus Christ our Lord. Amen.

— A Form of Prayer issued By Special Command
of his Majesty George III Imploring Divine assistance
against the King's unhappy deluded Subjects in America
now in rebellion against the Crown, 1776

The First Anniversary of Independence

The Revolution met with initial success, reflected in the following prayer, but after that settled down into a long and painstaking struggle with many times of despair and apparent failure.

Supremely great and infinitely glorious Lord our God! From everlasting to everlasting Thou art the same! Unchangeable in thy nature, in thy word, and in all thy works! Cloathed with light as with a garment, and with majesty as with a robe! Who makest the clouds thy chariot, and walkest upon the wings of the wind! Possessed of every adorable attribute and divine perfection!

We, thy unworthy but dependent children, assembled on this joyful occasion, humbly desire to approach the throne of thy grace, in and through the merit of thy coequal Son, our ever-blessed Saviour! For his sake, be pleased to pardon our manifold sins, and to blot out all our transgressions! Justify our persons through Immanuel's righteousness, and sanctify our natures by the powerful influences of thy most Holy Spirit! May we be wholly devoted to thy service, and live uniformly to thy praise!

With united hearts and uplifted voices, we render unfeigned thanks to thy name, O thou Sovereign Ruler of all worlds, for those numberless mercies wherewith we have been and continue to be visited! We adore thee for thy creating power, preserving goodness, and redeeming love! Suffer us never to forget any of thy favors, as we are altogether undeserving, even of the least! Particularly, O God! are the inhabitants of these States, on this day, under the strongest obligations to bless thy Name, for that Liberty, civil and religious, which they so fully enjoy! We would join the general body, and ascribe praise and thanksgiving to thy admirable majesty, for this auspicious Anniversary, a Day long to be remembered by us and future generations! A Day, whereon this extensive Continent was, by the representatives of a numerous and oppressed people, declared free and independent! Heaven approved the declaration, our arms were crowned with success, sweet peace hath visited our borders, the soldier once more became the citizen; Retiring, without regret, from stations of command, our military officers returned with cheerfulness to the several duties of domestic and tranquil life! Our ears are no more pierced with the confused noise of war, our eyes are no longer pained with the horrid spectacle of garments rol'd in blood. While we thus thankfully acknowledge thy reiterated favors in our political hemisphere, we beg leave also to mention thy providential smiles in crowning the Year with thy goodness, and causing thy paths to drop fatness; "Our pastures are cloathed with flocks, our fields are covered over with corn and with wheat, our husbandmen shout for joy, yea, they also sing."

That we may continue to enjoy these important blessings; Be pleased, O Lord, to visit all the nations of the earth, and incline their hearts to peace and love; shower down upon them thy heavenly grace; may they know thee as the King of Kings and Lord of Lords! In an especial manner, Do thou visit our land, graciously regard our country, protect and defend our infant, but hitherto highly favored empire, bless our Congress, smile upon each particular State of the Union; May those who are in authority rule in thy fear, prove a terror to evil doers and a praise to them who do well! As this is a period, O Lord, big with events, impenetrable by any human scrutiny, we fervently recommend to thy Fatherly notice that august Body, assembled in this city, who compose our Federal Convention; will it please thee, O thou Eternal I AM! to favour them from day to day with thy immediate presence; be thou their wisdom and their strength! Enable them to devise such measures as may prove happily instrumental for healing all divisions and promoting the good of the great whole; incline the hearts of all the people to receive with pleasure, combined with determination to carry into execution, whatever these thy servants may wisely recommend; That the United States of America may furnish the world with one example of a free and permanent government, which shall be the result of human and mutual deliberation, and which shall not, like all other governments, whether ancient or modern, spring out of mere chance or be established by force. May we triumph in the cheering prospect of being completely delivered from anarchy, and continue, under the influence of republican virtue, to partake of all the blessings of cultivated and civilized society! In tender mercy bless this Commonwealth, the President, Vice-President, and Supreme Executive Counsel, our Legislative Body, and the respective Judicial Departments!

Finally, we commend to thy paternal regard, all orders of men, all seminaries of useful learning, the Ministers of thy Gospel of every denomination, the Church of Christ, and all for whom we ought to pray. With heart-felt gratitude we anticipate the Glorious Era, when instead of the thorn shall come up the fir tree, instead of the briar shall come up the myrtle tree, and wisdom and knowledge shall be the stability of the times, both in church and state.

Prosper us, O Lord, Most Holy! for every dispensation of thy righteous Providence, for life, for death, for judgment, and the joys of Paradise — Humbly intreating thy gracious assistance, in suitably discharging all those duties enjoined us by thy word, and enforced by thy authority, we close this, our solemn address, by saying, as our Lord and Saviour Jesus Christ hath taught us —

Our Father, who art in Heaven; hallowed be thy name. Thy kingdom come. Thy will be done in earth, as it is in Heaven. Give us this day our daily bread. And forgive us our trespasses, as we forgive those who trespass against us. And lead us, not into temptation; but deliver us from evil. For thine is the kingdom, and the power and the glory, forever and ever. Amen.   — *William Rogers, 1777*

The Death of George Washington

AN ADDRESS AND A FORM OF PRAYER, Used in presence of the President, the Senate, and the House of Representatives of the United States; on the occasion of the solemnity produced by the Decease of General Washington, and preparatory to the delivery of an Oration in honour of the Deceased, by Major General Lee, on the 26th January 1800.

Forasmuch as it hath pleased Almighty God, in his wise providence, to take out of this world our beloved brother in Christ, and our ever honoured fellow-citizen, George Washington, formerly president of these United States; and, at the time of his decease, commander-in-chief of the armies of the same; let us bow down our souls in lowly submission under this afflictive dispensation. Let us offer up our thanksgivings and praises for the good example, for the exalted character, and for the signal services of the illustrious deceased. And let us pray that, through divine grace, we may make a religious improvement of the mournful event commemorated: so that after this transitory life shall be ended, we may rest with the spirits of just men made perfect; and finally may obtain unto the resurrection of life, through Jesus Christ our Lord; at whose second coming in glorious majesty to judge the world, the earth and sea shall give up their dead; and the corruptible bodies of those who sleep in him shall be changed; and made like unto his own glorious body; according to the mighty working whereby he is able to subdue all things unto himself.

Almighty God, with whom do live the spirits of those who depart hence in the Lord; and with whom the souls of the faithful, after they are delivered from the burthen of the flesh, are in joy and felicity: we give thee hearty thanks for the good examples of all those thy servants, who, having finished their course in faith, do now rest from their labours. And herein we especially adore and magnify thy name, for the eminent virtues and the illustrious actions of thy deceased servant, the late commander-in-chief of the armies of the United States. And while we acknowledge thy undeserved mercies, in having given him, at sundry times of difficulty and danger, to the councils and to the armies of this land; we pray that the present season of sensibility may impress us with due gratitude for the fatherly protection, which, through him, has been extended to us by thee, the Supreme Author of all good. May his memory be an incentive to those who shall come after him, in the presidency, in the command of armies, and in all the employments of the state. And may posterity, while they shall inherit the lustre of his name, enjoy the benefit of his life, in a continuance of the happy consequences of his labours; and in a succession of great and good men, to the glory of thy name, and the prosperity of thy people to the end of time. Finally, we pray that we, with all those thy servants who have departed this life in the true faith and fear of thy holy name, may rest in thee, and at last have our perfect consummation of bliss, both in body and soul, in thy eternal kingdom, through Jesus Christ our Lord. Amen.

O God, whose days are without end, and whose mercies are without number; make us, we beseech thee, sensible of the shortness and the uncertainty of this mortal life; and may we be resigned to thy will in every event of life and of death; and especially on the present occasion of general loss and grief. We implore the same for thy servant, the afflicted relict of the deceased; and for all allied to him in family or in friendship: beseeching thee that they may be sustained under their sorrows by the promises of thy Word; which encourages us not to sorrow as those who have no hope. And we pray for them, for ourselves, and for a whole mourning nation, that thy holy spirit may lead us through this vale of misery, in righteousness and holiness before thee, all our days; that when we shall have served thee in our generation, we may be gathered unto our fathers, having the testimony of a good conscience; in the communion of the Catholic Church; in the confidence of a certain faith; in the comfort of a reasonable, religious and holy hope; in favour with thee, our God; and in perfect charity with the world. All which we ask through Jesus Christ our Lord. Amen.

O God, who hast instructed us in thy Holy Word to render honour to whom it is due; we implore thy blessing on the celebration which is to follow. Support in the discharge of this duty thy servant, to whom it is committed. May this tribute of public gratitude and of private friendship obtain a reputation as extensive as that of the great name which it commemorates. May the inhabitants of this land, while with united hearts and voices they proclaim the praises of the assertor of their rights, the defender of their liberties and the vindicator of their laws, be perpetuating a call to virtuous and great achievements. And may all who, like our departed chief, of blessed memory, shall be eminent benefactors of mankind, like him also, find a grateful people honouring them in their lives and in their deaths. Which we ask through Jesus Christ our Lord. Amen.   — *William White, 1800*

On the 100th Anniversary of George Washington's Inauguration

O God, whose Name is excellent in all the earth, and whose glory is above the heavens; We bless thee for the great things thou hast done and art doing for the children of men. We consider the days of old, the years of ancient times, and unto thee do we give thanks. Moreover, we yield thee most high praise for the wonderful grace and virtue declared in all those thy children who have been the lights of the world in their several generations. For raising up thy servant George Washington, and giving him to be a leader and commander of thy people; for vouchsafing to him victory over kings, and for bestowing upon him many excellent gifts; for inclining the hearts of men in Congress assembled to wise choices, and for granting them vision of the days to come; for a settled constitution, and for equal laws; for freedom to do the thing that is right, and liberty to say the truth; for the spread of knowledge everywhere among us, and for the preservation of the faith; we bless and magnify thy holy Name, humbly beseeching thee to accept this our sacrifice of thanks and praise, through Jesus Christ our only Saviour and Redeemer. Amen.

— *Henry Codman Potter, 1889*

THE SLAVE TRADE AND CAMPAIGN FOR ABOLITION

Slavery was a divisive issue in the United States from the very beginning and there were many who argued that it was a Biblical institution. The Congress did, however, abolish the slave trade in 1808.

A Thanksgiving Prayer for the Abolition of the Slave Trade

Oh thou God of all nations upon the earth! we thank thee, that thou art *no respecter of persons,* and that *thou hast made of one blood all nation of men.* We thank thee, that thou hast appeared, in the fullness of time, in behalf of the nation from which most of the worshipping people, now before thee, are descended. We thank thee, that the *sun of righteousness* has at last shed morning beams upon them. *Rend thy heavens,* O Lord, and *come down* upon the earth; and grant that *the mountains,* which now obstruct the perfect day of thy goodness and mercy towards them, may *flow down at thy presence.* Send thy gospel we beseech thee, among them. May the nations, which now *sit in darkness,* behold and rejoice in its *light.* May *Ethiopia soon stretch out her hands unto thee,* and lay hold of the gracious promise of thy everlasting covenant. Destroy, we beseech thee, all the false religions which now prevail among them; and grant, that they may soon *cast* their *idols, to the moles and the bats* of the wilderness. O, hasten that glorious time, when the knowledge of the gospel of Jesus Christ, shall cover the *earth, as the waters cover the sea,* when *the wolf shall dwell with the lamb, and the leopard shall lie down with the kid, and the calf and the young lion and the fatling together, and a little child shall lead them* and when, *instead of the thorn, shall come up the fir tree, and, instead of the brier, shall come up the myrtle tree: and it shall be to the Lord for a name and for an everlasting sign that shall not be cut off.* We pray, O God, for all our friends and benefactors in Great Britain, as well as in the United States: reward them, we beseech thee, with blessings upon earth, and prepare them to enjoy the fruits of their kindness to us, in thy everlasting kingdom in heaven; and dispose us, who are assembled in thy presence, to be always thankful for thy mercies, and to act as becomes a people who owe so much to thy goodness. We implore thy blessing, O God, upon the President, and all who are in authority in the United States. Direct them by thy wisdom, in all their deliberations, and O save thy people from the calamities of war. Give peace in our day we beseech thee, O thou *God of peace!* and grant, that this highly favoured country may continue to afford a safe and peaceful retreat from the calamities of war and slavery, for ages yet to come. We implore all these blessings and mercies, only in the name of thy beloved Son, Jesus Christ, our Lord. And now, O Lord, we desire, with angels and archangels, and all the company of heaven, ever more to praise thee, saying, *"Holy, holy. holy. Lord God Almighty;* the whole earth is full of thy glory." — *Absalom Jones, 1808*

A Modern Prayer for Peace and Justice
Based on Absalom Jones's prayer

Most holy God, Creator of all mankind, we thank you that you make no distinctions among your people and that you have made of one blood all nations and races on earth. We thank you for bringing us together in the fullness of time in this nation and for leading us year by year toward the overcoming of our human divisions. Rend the heavens, O Lord, and come down upon the earth; and grant that the mountains which now obstruct the perfect day of your goodness and mercy towards us may flow down at your presence. Send your gospel among us. May the peoples of the earth see and rejoice in its light. Help us to overcome the ignorance and prejudice that separate us and to grow in understanding of your presence among those who do not speak as we speak or worship as we worship. Hasten that glorious time, when the knowledge of your love shall cover the earth, as the waters cover the sea, when the wolf shall dwell with the lamb, and the leopard shall lie down with the kid, and the calf and the young lion and the fatling together, and a little child shall lead us and when, instead of the thorn, shall come up the fir tree, and, instead of the brier, shall come up the myrtle tree: and it shall be to the Lord for a name and for an everlasting sign that shall not be cut off.

We pray, O God, for all those who work for peace and justice in every part of the world: strengthen and uphold them in your goodness and turn our hearts to support them with our prayers and generous giving of our time and treasure. We ask your blessing and guidance, O God, on the President, the Congress, and all who are in authority in the United States. Direct them by your wisdom, in all their deliberations, and save your people from the calamities of war and violence. Give peace in our day we beseech you, O God of peace, and grant that this greatly favored country may continue to provide a place of peace and security and opportunity for ages yet to come. All these gifts we ask in the name of your Son, Jesus Christ our Lord. Amen.   — *Christopher Webber*

THE WAR OF 1812

The War of 1812 was an American sideshow to the Napoleonic wars being waged in Europe. Exasperated by the British blockade of French ports and by British kidnapping of American sailors, the United States declared war on England. The two and a half years of war proved inconclusive; although the British burned the White House, American forces won victories in naval battles on the Great Lakes and, when the war was technically over, at New Orleans. A peace treaty was signed in December 1814, and the President set aside the second Thursday of April 1815 as a day of national thanksgiving for the restoration of peace. Bishop John Henry Hobart provided the following prayers to be used on that day in the Episcopal Diocese of New York.

O God who art the blessed and only Potentate, the King of Kings, and Lord of Lords, the Almighty Ruler of nations, we adore and magnify thy glorious name for all the great things which thou hast done for us. We render thee thanks for the goodly heritage which thou hast given us; for the civil and religious privileges which we enjoy; and for the multiplied manifestations of thy favour towards us. Especially, we devoutly thank thee for putting it into the hearts of the nations to terminate the wars which have desolated the earth; and for restoring to our country and to the world, the blessings of peace. Thou hast not dealt with us, O God, according to our sins; thou hast not rewarded us after our wickednesses. It was not our arm that saved us, but thy right hand, and thine arm, and the light of thy countenance, because thou hadst a favour unto us. Therefore, not unto us, O Lord, not unto us but unto thy name be given the glory. Grant that we may show forth our thankfulness for these thy mercies, by living in the reverence of thy almighty power and dominion, in humble reliance on thy goodness and mercy, and in holy obedience to thy righteous laws. Preserve, we beseech thee, to our country and to all the nations of the earth the blessings of peace. May the Kingdom of the Prince of Peace come, and reigning in the hearts and lives of men, unite them in holy fellowship; that so their only strife may be, who shall show forth with most humble and holy fervour, the praises of him who hath loved them, and made them Kings and Priests unto God. We implore thy blessing on all in authority over us, that all things may be so ordered and settled by their endeavours, upon the best and surest foundation, that peace and happiness, truth and justice, religion and piety, may be established among us for all generations. O Lord, we beseech thee to shed the quickening influences of thy Holy Spirit on all the people of this land. May we fear to abuse the blessings of prosperity to luxury and licentiousness, to irreligion and vice; lest we provoke thee in just judgment, to visit our offences with a rod, and our sins with scourges. And while thy unmerited and unexpected goodness to us, O God of our salvation, leads us to repentance, may we offer ourselves, our souls and bodies, a living sacrifice to thee, who hast preserved and redeemed us, through Jesus Christ our Lord; on whose merits and mediation alone we humbly rely for the forgiveness of our sins and the acceptance of our services; and who liveth and reigneth with the Father and the Holy Ghost, ever one God, world without end. Amen.   —*John Henry Hobart, 1815*

1861–1865: THE AMERICAN CIVIL WAR

Prayers of the Confederacy

On November 1, 1860, on the eve of the election that brought Abraham Lincoln to the White House and convinced the southern states that they could not remain in union, the Rt. Rev. Thomas F. Davis of South Carolina issued "A Prayer for Guidance" for use when the legislature was in session. The "Prayer for the Confederacy" was published in a church newspaper, The Southern Churchman, *but it was not completely new. It had been written by the Archbishop of Canterbury at the end of the sixteenth century for use during the war between Spain and England and was "slightly altered" to adapt it to the circumstance of the southern dioceses.*

A Prayer for Guidance

O, Almighty and eternal God, who dwelling in the heavens, rulest over all and governest the nations upon earth, dispensing to all their destinies according to Thy holy and righteous will, we acknowledge our entire dependence upon Thee. We humble ourselves before Thee, under a deep sense of our unworthiness; and awful apprehension of Thy divine majesty. Be merciful to us, O God of our salvation, in this our day of trial and necessity. Hear our prayer and let our cry come unto Thee. Look down from heaven, we beseech Thee, upon the people of these United States: visit and enlighten their hearts; order their will and affections and overrule all their purposes to the ends of truth and justice, of righteousness and peace. We beseech Thee especially to bless the people of this state. Thou, O God, sittest upon the throne judging right. Our hearts are open unto Thee. To Thee we make our prayer. Pardon the sins of Thy people and direct all their ways. Make them obedient to Thy Blessed will and acceptable in Thy sight, that so we may be Thy people and Thou may'st be our God. Endue the general assembly of this state, now in session, with the spirit of wisdom, of courage and of a sound mind. Sanctify and rule their hearts by the mighty power of the Holy Ghost. Save them from error and inspire and guide their counsels that so their decisions may be righteous in Thy sight and such as Thou wilt bless, prosper and establish. Bless our governor and all others in authority. Give unto them wisdom and strength that all their acts may tend only to the promotion of Thy glory and the happiness of Thy people. And, O God, Father of our Lord Jesus Christ and

Redeemer of all mankind, pour Thy spirit upon all orders
and degrees of men among us and subdue their will to the
blessed Gospel of the Son of God; so that Thy people may
be adorned with that righteousness which becometh a nation
and blessed by Thee forever more. Through Jesus Christ our
Lord to whom with Thee and the Holy Ghost be glory and
dominion world without end. Amen.

— Thomas F. Davis, 1860

A Prayer for the Confederacy

O eternal God, in power most mighty, in strength most glorious, without whom the horse and chariot is in vain prepared
against the day of battle, vouchsafe, we beseech Thee, from
thy high throne of majesty, to hear and receive the hearty and
humble prayer which, on bended knees, we the people of thy
pasture and sheep of thy hand, unfeignedly acknowledging
thy might and our own weakness now pour out before Thee,
on behalf of these Confederate States, their rulers and their
valiant men of war, who, by Thee inspired, have put their
lives in their hands, and at this time do oppose themselves
against the malice and violence of such as bear a mortal hate
against us. Arise, O Lord, and stand up, we pray Thee, to
help and defend them. Be Thou their Captain to go in and
out before them and to lead them in their way. Teach Thou
their fingers to fight and their hands to make battle. The generals and chieftains bless with the spirit of wisdom, counsel,
and discretion; the soldiers with minds ready to perform and
execute. Gird them all with strength and pour out upon them
the spirit of courage. Give them in the day of battle, hearts
like the hearts of lions, invincible and fearless against evil, but
terrible to such as come out against them. When the enemy
doth rage and danger approach, be Thou, O Lord, a rock of

salvation and a tower of defence unto them. Break the enemy's weapons. As smoke vanisheth, so let their enemies be scattered, and let such as hate them flee before them. Thou seest, O Lord, the malice of our adversaries, how they bear a tyrannous hate against us, continually vexing and troubling us who fain would live at peace. Stir up, therefore, O Lord, thy strength, and avenge our just quarrel. Turn the sword of our enemy upon his own head, and cause his delight in war to be his own destruction. As Thou hast dealt with him heretofore, so now scatter his forces, and spoil his mighty ships wherein he trusteth. So shall we, the people of thy inheritance, give praise unto thy name, and for thy great mercy give thanks unto thee in the great congregation. Yea, the world shall know and the nations shall understand, to the praise of thy glory, that Thou alone defendest them that trust in Thee and givest victory to nations. Hear us, O Lord, our strength, in these our prayers, for Jesus Christ his sake. Amen.

— *The Southern Churchman, 1860*

Prayer of a Southern Bishop

O Lord God, that dwellest in the heavens and who reignest over all the kingdoms of men, we praise and bless Thy name that, in our troubles and perils, Thou hast stood on our side and pleaded for us against them that rose up against us. It was Thy hand, O Lord, and the help of Thy mercy that relieved us. Thou, O Lord, didst blast the designs of our enemies with the breath of Thy displeasure, and to Thee we ascribe the praise and honor of our present safety. Perpetuate Thy mercies to us; let a guard of Holy Angels stand round about us and about all Thy people, like the hills for our defense and safety, that we may be inaccessible by all the attempts of our enemies. Let us receive the blessings which our Lord Jesus Christ left unto

His church, even the peace of God the Father, God the Son, and God the Holy Ghost, to whom be all honor and glory, now and forever. Amen.   —*Stephen Elliot, 1863*

For the Nation

This prayer was offered by the United States Senate Chaplain in the commemoration of Independence Day 1861, in the first days of the Civil War.

Almighty and everlasting God, be not angry with us for our sins, which we only confess and deplore; but pardon our offenses and extend to us Thy favor. We thank Thee for Thy goodness on this anniversary of the nation, a day tenfold more precious by reason of our present troubles, and sacred to the heart for the ever memorable Declaration of our fathers, in which Thou didst begin more openly to give us a name among the nations of the earth. We thank Thee for all Thy manifold and abundant mercies hitherto to make our nation exceedingly great and glorious; but now disasters have befallen us and darkness broods in the land. And now we ask Thy mercy as the Senate is convening at a most momentous crisis of our history. Give to Thy servants all needed help. Add to their deliberations wisdom and unanimity, and profit and speed to their conclusion. Bless Thy servant, the President of the United States, our veteran Commander-in-Chief, and all that have functions in the civil and military power. May the angel of Thy presence walk in the Cabinet and in the Congress and in the camp, to go before, to purify, and to direct the now greatly and universally-awakened love of country. And we beseech Thee to guide us, to overrule and order all things, and so to cause that nothing shall fail, that the disorders of the land may be speedily healed, that peace and concord may prevail, that truth and righteousness may be established, and that Thy Church and Kingdom may flourish in a larger peace and prosperity, for Thy Son, our Saviour, Jesus Christ's sake. Amen.   — *Byron Sunderland, July 4, 1861*

Prayers for the Union

The next two prayers are from a collection of prayers issued by various bishops of the Episcopal Church for use in their dioceses.

O Lord God Almighty, the Creator and Preserver of the Universe, by whose Providence the nations of the earth are governed and sustained, we humbly desire to prostrate our souls before Thy Majesty in this time of trial, when the sad calamity of civil war has been appointed to chasten us for our innumerable sins of pride, profanity and irreligion. O Lord, in wrath, remember mercy. Restrain the madness of human passion, the arm of cruel violence, and the effusion of blood. Protect our friends and brethren, who have gone forth at the call of our government, to fight the battles of the country. And grant, in thine infinite mercy, that this mournful conflict may soon be ended, and our land restored again to prosperity and peace. We ask this blessing at Thy hand, who art the only Giver of all victory, in the name and for the sake of Thy son, Jesus Christ, our Lord. Amen.

— *John Henry Hopkins, Bishop of Vermont*

Almighty and everlasting God, our only refuge in the hour of peril, look with pity we beseech thee upon the desolations of our beloved country. Our sins have called for Thy righteous judgments. We confess our guilt and bewail our transgressions. O Lord, in thy judgment remember mercy. Take away from us all hatred and strife. Spare us for Thy church's sake, for the sake of Thy dear Son, from the calamities of civil war. Give Thy Holy Spirit to our rulers that under Thy protection they may save this great nation from anarchy and ruin. Preserve them from all blindness, pride, prejudice, and enmity. Give unto the people unity, a love of justice, and an understanding heart. Restrain the wrath of man and save the effusion of blood. Bring again the blessings of peace and grant unto us a heart to serve Thee and walk before Thee in holiness all the days of our life. These things which we are not worthy to ask, we humbly beg for the sake of Thy dear Son, our Lord and Savior Jesus Christ. Amen.

— *Henry Whipple, Bishop of Minnesota*

In Time of War

O God, who art the blessed and only Potentate, the King of kings and Lord of lords, doing according to thy will in the army of heaven, and among the inhabitants of the earth, who didst choose thy servant Cornelius, the soldier, a devout man, and one that feared thee, as the first fruits of the Gospel among the Gentiles; We humbly implore thy blessing upon all officers and soldiers (*or sailors*) composing the army (*or navy*) of the United States. Fit them, we beseech thee, for their several duties, and guard them as against all dangers and temptations, so especially against those peculiar to their respective stations. May they be men fearing thee, eschewing evil and doing good; save them from all unchristian feelings of ill-will, revenge and violence; from all bitterness, wrath, and clamor and evil speaking; and from all offenses against Christian purity and sobriety. Infuse into them a love of order, good discipline and obedience to authority. Make them instrumental to the preserving and strengthening of the peace, tranquility and welfare of our country. May they never be called to battle but in a righteous cause, and when they go forth to the fight, may thy shield protect them and thy mighty arm assist them. More especially we pray for the grace of thy Holy Spirit, that by the purity of their faith, the godliness of their lives and their fidelity to the obligations of the Christian covenant, they may manfully fight under Christ's banner against sin, the world and the devil, and continue his faithful soldiers and servants unto their lives' end; and, finally, may they receive the crown of glory which the Lord, the righteous Judge, will give to him that overcometh. All which we ask in the Name and for the sake of the Captain of our salvation thy Son, Jesus Christ. Amen. — *Alonzo Potter*

During Civil War

O Almighty God, who art a strong tower of defence to those who put their trust in thee, whose power no creature is able to resist; We make our humble cry to thee in this hour of our country's need. Thy property is always to have mercy. Deal not with us according to our sins, neither reward us according to our iniquities; but stretch forth the right hand of thy Majesty and be our defence for thy name's sake. Have pity upon our brethren who are in arms against the constituted authorities of the land, and show them the error of their way. Shed upon the counsels of our rulers the spirit of wisdom and moderation and firmness, and unite the hearts of our people in upholding the supremacy of law, and the cause of justice and peace. Abate the violence of passion; banish pride and prejudice from every heart and incline us all to trust in thy righteous providence, and to be ready for every duty. And O, that in thy great mercy, thou wouldest hasten the return of unity and concord to our borders, and so order all things that

peace and happiness, truth and justice, religion and piety may
be established among us for all generations. These things and
whatever else thou shalt see to be necessary and convenient
for us, we humbly beg through the merits and mediation of
Jesus Christ our Lord and Savior. Amen

— *Alonzo Potter, Bishop of Pennsylvania, c. 1862*

1863: A Day of National Thanksgiving

*The Battle of Gettysburg (July 1–3, 1863), is generally recog-
nized as the turning point in the American Civil War. Having
defeated the Union Army in Virginia, General Robert E. Lee
decided to strike into the north in hope of destroying northern
morale and encouraging European support for the southern
cause. After three days of fighting in which nearly a third of
those on both sides were killed or injured, General Lee was
forced to withdraw. President Abraham Lincoln decreed a
day of National Thanksgiving, Praise and Prayer to Almighty
God, and Episcopal Bishop Horatio Potter of New York sent
the following prayers to all his clergy for use on that day,
August 6, 1863.*

O Almighty God, the Sovereign Commander of all the World,
in whose hand is power and might, which none is able to
withstand; we bless and magnify Thy great and glorious
Name for the late happy success of our efforts in defence
of our Country, the whole glory whereof we ascribe to Thee
who art the only Giver of Victory. And we beseech Thee, give
us grace to improve these great mercies to Thy glory, the advancement of Thy Gospel, the honour of our Country, and,
as much as in us lieth, to the good of all Mankind. And, we
beseech Thee, give us such a sense of these Thy mercies, as
may engage us to a true thankfulness, such as may appear in

our lives, by an humble, holy and obedient walking before Thee all our days, through Jesus Christ, our Lord; to Whom, with Thee and the Holy Spirit, be all glory and honour, world without end. Amen.

Almighty God, whose kingdom is everlasting and power infinite; Have mercy upon the whole Church, and so rule the hearts of those who are in chief power and authority in this Nation, that they, knowing Whose ministers they are, may above all things seek Thy honor and glory; and that we, and all those who are subject to their administration of the Constitution and Laws by which they and we are governed, duly considering whose authority they bear, may faithfully serve, honor and humbly obey the law of the land by them administered and executed, in Thee and for Thee, according to Thy blessed Word and Ordinance: through Jesus Christ our Lord, Who, with Thee and the Holy Ghost, liveth and reigneth ever, world without end. Amen.

Most gracious God, we humbly beseech Thee, as for the people of these United States in general, so especially for all those who in Council or in the Field shall be called on to assist in restoring to peaceful and orderly course the affairs of this whole Nation; that Thou wouldst be pleased to direct and prosper all their consultations, and to guide and further their proceedings, to the advancement of Thy glory, the good of Thy Church, the safety, honor and welfare of Thy people; that all things may he so ordered and settled by their endeavors, upon the best and surest foundations, that peace and happiness, truth and justice, religion and piety may be established among us for all generations. These and all other necessaries, for them, for us, and Thy whole Church, we humbly beg in the Name and Mediation of Jesus Christ, our most blessed Lord and Saviour. Amen.

O merciful God and Heavenly Father, who hast taught us in Thy Word that Thou dost not willingly afflict or grieve the children of men; We humbly beseech Thee of Thy goodness to comfort and succor all those who are at this time suffering in the miserable calamities brought upon this Nation by sedition and civil war. Mercifully vouchsafe supplies of spiritual strength and consolation to the wounded, sick and dying, and raise up friends for them in their need. Be a Father to the fatherless, and a Husband to the widow. Furnish shelter to the homeless, sustenance to the impoverished, support to the bereaved and destitute. Lighten the bonds of those who are captives or in prison. Give all, in their several visitations, a right understanding of themselves and of Thy threats and promises, that they may neither cast away their confidence in Thee, nor place it anywhere but in Thee. Relieve the distressed, protect the innocent, and awaken the guilty; and forasmuch as Thou alone bringest light out of darkness, and good out of evil, make the manifold forms of human suffering now darkening our land effectual for the conversion of many souls to Thee, that among us fruits meet for repentance may be abundantly brought forth, and that the glory of Thy grace may be made known among all nations, now and forevermore; through Jesus Christ our Lord. Amen.

Almighty God and most merciful Father, who, in Thy wise and loving Providence toward mankind, hast ordained Powers for the administration of civil authority, to rule and govern in Thy Name the people on the earth committed to their charge; and hast commanded all in their several stations, to render unto them true and due obedience in Thy fear, even for conscience' sake, withholding neither honor, nor tribute, nor custom, nor orderly subjection and submission; and hast furthermore enjoined Thy people to offer unto Thee for such civil rulers all Supplications, Prayers, Intercessions and

Thanksgiving: We, remembering such Thy commands and injunctions, do now most humbly approach Thee to render due Praise, Honor and Thanksgiving for the mercies of late vouchsafed to this Nation, by the good success of those entrusted with its government in the suppression of the grievous rebellion by which the very being of the Nation, and all orderly administration of its laws and institutions, have been in peril of utter ruin and extinction. We acknowledge, O Lord, that Thou hast done wonderful things in our behalf, of the least of which we are not worthy. Whereas our deservings have been only wrath and condemnation, and have most justly brought upon us the miseries and sorrows by which, as a nation, and far and wide throughout the homes and households of the land, we have been afflicted; Thou, in the midst of wrath, hast remembered mercy, and hast not caused us to be utterly confounded and dismayed, but opened for us a door of deliverance by the faithful service of brave men fighting the battles of their country on land and sea in behalf of the Law and Order which are from Thee, in breaking which man fighteth against Thee, and in maintaining which, at whatever hazard or extremity, the humblest citizen, in his place, is bound to do Thee service. For the signal and effective victories with which Thou hast vouchsafed to reward their efforts, we render Thee hearty thanks and praise; beseeching Thee to continue Thy most gracious protection to our armies and fleets, and to use them as Thy instruments for the restoration of peace, good order and godly quietness in the land. And humbly we entreat Thee to give to us, and to all this People, grace to use these Thy great mercies shown toward us to the furtherance of Thy glory, the advancement of Thy Gospel, the honor of our country, and as much as in us lieth the good of all mankind. Stir up our hearts, O Lord, to a true thankfulness, such as may appear in our lives by a humble, holy and obedient walking before Thee all our days: Through Jesus Christ our Lord, to Whom with Thee, O Father, and Thee, O Holy Ghost, as for all Thy services, so in particular for those for which this day, with all this Nation, we return Thee thanks, be all glory and honor, world without end. Amen.

Almighty God, who hast in all ages showed forth Thy power in the protection of every nation and people faithfully professing thy holy and eternal Truth, and putting their sure trust in Thee; We yield Thee our unfeigned thanks and praise for all Thy public mercies, and more especially for those now recently vouchsafed to this Nation, in its need: Wherefore not unto us, O Lord, not unto us, but unto Thy Name be ascribed all honor and glory, in all Churches of the Saints, from generation to generation: through Jesus Christ our Lord.

— *Horatio Potter, 1863*

THE DEATH OF ABRAHAM LINCOLN, APRIL 1865

Bishop Simpson's Prayer at the White House

Matthew Simpson, a close friend of the president, was present as he lay dying and offered a prayer transcribed by one of those present, first indirectly and then more directly.

In the course of his prayer the Bishop said that in the hands of God were the issues of life and death. Our sins had called for his wrath to descend upon us as individuals and as a community. For the sake of our blessed Redeemer, forgiveness was asked for all our transgressions, and that all our iniquities, may be washed away. While we bow under this sad bereavement which has caused a wide spread gloom, not only in this circle but over the entire land; an invocation was made that all might submit to God's holy will. Thanks were returned for the gift of such a man as our Heavenly Father had just taken from us, and for the many virtues which distinguished all his transactions; for the integrity, honesty and transparency of character bestowed upon him, and for having given him counsellors to guide our nation through periods of unprecedented sorrow. He was permitted to live to behold the breaking of the clouds which over-hung our national sky, and the disintegration of the rebellion. Going up the mount he beheld the land of promise, with its beauty and happiness, and the glorious destiny reserved for us as a nation.

Thanks were also returned that his arm was strengthened and wisdom and firmness given to his heart to pen a declaration of emancipation by which were broken the chains of millions of the human race. God be thanked that the assassin who struck down the Chief Magistrate had not the hand to again bind the suffering and oppressed. The name of the beloved dead would ever be identified with all that is great and glorious with humanity on earth. God grant that all who stand here entrusted with the administration of public affairs may have the power, strength and wisdom to complete the work of His Servant so gloriously begun, and may the successor of the deceased President not bear the sword in vain. God grant that strength may be given to him and to our military to perfect victory, and to complete the contest now nearly closed. May the spirit of rebellion soon pass away. May the last vestige of slavery, which caused the rebellion, be driven from our land. God grant that the sun may shine on a free people from the Atlantic to the Pacific, and from the lakes to the Gulf. May He not only safely lead us through the struggle, but give us peace with all nations of the earth. Give us hearts to deal justly with them, and give them hearts to deal justly with us, so that universal peace may reign on earth.

We raise our hearts to Thee, to plead that Thy blessing may descend on the family of the deceased. God bless the weeping widow as in her broken-heartedness she bows under a sad stroke more than she can bear. Encircle her in Thy own arms. God, be gracious with the children left behind him. Endow his sons with wisdom from on high; endow them with great usefulness. May they appreciate the patriotic example and virtues of their father, and walk in his footsteps. We pray Thee to make the assassination of personal profit to our hearts, while by the remains of the deceased, whom we had called a friend, do Thou grant us peace and repentance of our sins. So that at the end of life we may be gathered where assassins are not found, where sorrow and sickness never come; but all gather in peace and love around the Father's throne in glory. We pray Thee that our Republic may be made the stronger for this blow. While here we pledge ourselves to set our faces as a flint against every form of opposition which may rise up for its destruction; so that we, the children, may enjoy the blessed advantages of a government delivered from our fathers.   *— Matthew Simpson, 1865*

The Rev. Dr. Boynton's Prayer

Almighty God, who dost inhabit eternity, while we appear but for a little moment and then vanish away, we adore Thy eternal name. Infinite in power and majesty and greatly to be feared art Thou. All earthly distinctions disappear in Thy presence, and we come before Thy throne simply as men — fallen men, condemned alike by Thy law, and justly cut off, through sin, from communion with Thee. But through Thy infinite mercy, a new way of access has been opened through Thy Son, and consecrated by His blood. We come in that all worthy name and plead the promise of pardon and acceptance through Him. By the imposing solemnities of this scene, we are carried back to the hour when the nation heard and shuddered at hearing that Abraham Lincoln was dead — was murdered. We would bow ourselves submissively to Him by whom that awful stroke fell on the country in the very hour of its triumph, and hushed all its shouts of victory to one voiceless sorrow. The Lord gave and the Lord hath taken away. Blessed is the name of the Lord.

The shadow of that death has not yet passed from the heart of the nation, as this National testimonial bears witness to-day. The gloom thrown from these surrounding emblems of death is fringed, we know, with the glory of a great triumph, and the light of a great and good man's memory. Still, O Lord, may this hour bring to us the proper warning. Be you also ready, for in such an hour as ye think not, the Son of Man cometh. Any one of us may be called as suddenly as he whom we mourn. We worship Thee as the God of our Fathers. Thou didst trace for them a path over the trackless sea, and bring them to these shores, bearing with them the seed of a vast dominion. We thank Thee that the life-power of the young nation they planted received from Thee such energy, guidance, and protection; that it spread rapidly over the breadth of the Continent, carrying with it Christian liberty, churches, schools, and all the blessings of a Christian civilization. We thank Thee that the progress of the true American life has been irresistible, because sustained by Thy eternal counsels and Thy almighty power, and because the might of God was in this national life we have seen it sweeping all opposition away, grinding great systems and parties to powder, and breaking in pieces the devices of men, and Thou hast raised up for it heroic defenders in every hour of peril. We thank Thee, O strong Defender.

And when treason was hatching its plots, and massing its armies, then, O God of Israel, who didst bring David from the sheepfold, Thou gavest one reared in the humble cabin to become the hope and stay of this great people in their most perilous hour, to shield them in disaster, and lead them to final victory. We thank Thee that Thou gavest us an honest man, simple hearted, and loving as a child, but with a rugged strength that needed only culture and discipline. Thanks be to God that this discipline was granted him through stern public trial, domestic sorrow, and Thy solemn providence, till the mere politician was overshadowed by the nobler growth of his moral and spiritual nature, till he came, as we believe, into sympathy with Christ, and saw that we could succeed only by doing justice. Then, inspired by Thee he uttered those words of power which changed three millions of slaves into men — the great act which has rendered his name forever illustrious, and secured the triumph of our cause. We think of him almost as the prophet of his era. Thou didst make that honest, great-hearted man the central figure of his age, setting upon his goodness, upon his moral grandeur, the seal of Thine approval and the crown of victory. We bless Thee that he did not die until assured of victory, until he knew that his great work was done, and he had received all the honor that the earth could bestow, and then we believe Thou didst give him a martyr's crown. We thank Thee that we have this hope for the illustrious dead.

Great reason have we also to thank Thee that such was the enduring strength of our institutions, that they received no perceptible shock from the death even of such a man and in such an hour, and that Thou didst provide for that perilous moment one whose strength was sufficient to receive and bear the weight of government, and who, we trust, will work out the great problem of Christian freedom to its full solution, and build this great people into one inseparable whole. We thank Thee that the Representatives of the nation have come to sit today in the shadow of Abraham Lincoln's tomb, to express once more their now chastened sorrow. May they all reconsecrate themselves to those principles which made him worthy to be remembered thus; and then a redeemed and transfigured land will be a fitting monument to him and for them.

Endow the President with wisdom equal to his great responsibilities, that the blessings of a whole nation may also be given to him. May his advisers, our judges, and our legislators be constantly instructed by Thee. May Thy blessing rest on the officers of the army and navy, by whose skill and courage our triumph was won; upon our soldiers and sailors, upon our people, and on those who are struggling on toward a perfect manhood; Bless these eminent men, the honored representatives of foreign powers. Remember the sovereigns and people whom they represent. We thank Thee that peace reigns with them as with us. May it continue until the nations shall learn war no more.

Remember Abraham Lincoln's widow and family. Comfort them in their sore bereavement. May they be consoled to know how much the father and husband is loved and honored still. Give Divine support to the distinguished orator of the day. May he so speak as to impress the whole nation's mind. Prepare us to live as men in this age should, that we may be received into Thy heavenly kingdom; and to Thy name shall be the praise and the glory for evermore. Amen.

A Prayer at a Service of National Penitence and Renewal after President Lincoln's Death

Almighty God, thou art our fathers' God. They trusted in thee, and were not put to shame. In times of trouble we have proved thee, and found thy promises yea and amen. None that put their trust in thee in a just cause shall fail. For, though "clouds and darkness are round about thee," justice and judgment are the habitation of thy throne. And we rejoice that thou art now making the dark clouds to part. We see the bright shining of justice between. Yet thou hast reached thine hand forth, and plucked from the highest place in this nation, and from the highest place in our admiration and affection, thy servant, the late President of these United States; and we are as a tree whose branch the storm hath wrenched off. We know our loss; and we believe that thy providence hath chastisement and condemnation.

Yet thou hast, in thy wrath, remembered mercy. Thou didst ordain him to be thy servant of justice. Thou didst temper his heart to integrity, moderation, and love. In a stormy time, between a divided people with strong passions, turbulent and deadly, thou didst plant him. and to the end maintain in him temperance, fortitude, self-denial, patience, meekness, gentleness, justice, and love. And thou didst accomplish thy work by him, and didst leave his name an honor and a glory to this people, shining out brighter and brighter every day hitherward, and yet shining out bright as the stars thitherward.

And now, O Lord, our God, thou hast, in thy providence, by the voice of our chief magistrate, convoked us today, that we might repent before God of our sins, confessing them; and that we might improve this day as a day of humiliation and prayer. Vouchsafe, we beseech thee, to this great nation, a profound sense of their sinfulness. Give life to the national conscience; give honesty to this people. May they sit in judgment on their past, and be sterner in judgment upon themselves than can any other people be upon them.

We confess that we have been a people puffed up by prosperity. We have been made arrogant by our strength. We have been corrupted by the readiness and abundance of our wealth. And those favors that have been meant for our nourishing we have prostituted to luxury, and made to serve as instruments for our degradation unto selfishness. Nay, we have been willing to employ our strength for oppression; we have heeded not the cry of the poor; — we have contented ourselves with securing our own exceeding great prosperity, not only in indifference to those that suffered, but in contempt of them.

We confess the sin of the Christian ministry, and of the church. They have not been faithful to the trust committed to them. They have not stood as perpetual judges and condemners of wrong in the midst of this people. We confess that the gospel hath had its light hidden. We confess that there has not been that testimony which there should have been. Nor do we seek to excuse ourselves. We confess that the North, which loved liberty, hath hidden its love of liberty, loving better other things. We, too, have taken gain of oppression, and we, too, have sought quiet at the sacrifice of principle; and we confess that in these thunderous strokes and dark days of storm we are receiving punishment. For we have been guilty concerning our brother. The blood that cries from the ground cries in part against us; and blood hath atoned for blood.

Now, O Lord, our God, we beseech thee that thou wilt grant that this whole people may confess their sins. May we acknowledge that we have been false to the principles of our government; false to the truths of our faith; false to our manhood, to our Christianity, to God and to man; and may we understand that thou hast been angry with us, though now thy face is clearing away, and thou art tempering judgment with mercy. We desire to be penetrated with a sense of our deserving, and desire to confess that our judgments have been fewer than our sins. And we beseech thee that we may be more anxious to confess our own sins than to charge their sins upon those that have sinned grievously. And we beseech thee that the time past may be sufficient. May this people, out of the judgments through which they have gone, see this truth of God, sublime as the throne of eternity, that God loves justice. And may we not seek any further to deceive. Thou art not mocked; and whatever a nation sows, that shall it reap. May we not seek to sow inequalities, and injustice, and dominance of strength over weakness. May we sow righteousness, and justice, and liberty, and truth throughout the whole of this land, and may they spring up and bring forth fruit an hundredfold.

Be pleased to bless the President of these United States, and all that in authority are associated with him. Grant that his mind may be illumined from on high. May he see what things are just and right; and what things are merciful. And wilt thou give him such counsel that he shall ordain judgment and mercy; both of them in the fear of God, both of them in accordance with thy Spirit.

And we beseech of thee that thou wilt grant thy blessing to rest on the army and navy of these United States. We thank thee for the fidelity of our men. We thank thee that so many live, though so many have afflicted our hearts in death. Be pleased to bless those that are wounded and maimed, those that are sick, those that are among strangers. Grant, we beseech thee, that all their afflictions may be blessed to them spiritually and temporally.

Remember, we beseech thee, all those that lately have been enslaved, but that now are free. We thank thee for their good conduct. Thou hast had thoughts of mercy toward them. Wilt thou still, in thy providence, ordain industry, and honesty, and frugality among them. And grant that they may prove their worthiness to be citizens, and be established immutably on the ground of citizenship.

Be pleased, we beseech thee, to bless our enemies. May those that of late have been in arms against us come up in remembrance before thee. How great are their sufferings! How great have been the desolations of war in their midst! Lord, may their mischiefs be repaired. Grant that their prosperity may be rebuilded once more. And may brethren begin to call each other by names of love, and not by inimical names. And grant that the hands already beginning to reach across the wastes of war may be clasped not only in compact of friendship, but in the fealty of justice and liberty. And grant that the whole citizenship of this great nation, now reunited, may never be severed again. May this great people be one; with no mischief in their bosom; with no cause of fermentation; with no taint or tendency to decay. May all love each other, because all love God supremely. May the weak be strengthened by the strong, and the ignorant be illumined by the wise.

And may all mankind come up in remembrance before thee. And today may we feel the bond that connects us with our fellows in all the earth. And may this nation, strengthened, repaired, made great, be great, not for rapine and selfishness, but for justice; and may the influence which it exerts among the nations of the earth be for liberty, and truth, and purity. And may all men learn to love this people, because God is in their midst, and they are clothed with the beauty of holiness.

And now, grant thy blessing to rest upon thy servant, who has been called by his fellow-citizens to speak in their behalf this day. Clothe him with power. Make his words mighty. Grant that a blessing may go forth with them, and that they may shake down, as dew from perfumed shrubs, joy and profit upon us.

And grant that through life we may have thee for our God; and, dying, we may find thee near. And, when no longer we can see thee, may we reach out our hands and find thee leading us through death to immortality and glory. For Christ Jesus' sake. Amen.   —*Henry Ward Beecher, 1867*

Remembering the Civil War in 1907

At the unveiling of the equestrian statue of General Stuart that stands today on Monument Avenue in Richmond, Virginia.

We ask, O Lord, our God, Thy blessing upon the service in which we are about to engage. "Pour down upon us the abundance of Thy mercy, forgiving us those things whereof our conscience is afraid and giving us those good things which we are not worthy to ask but through Thy Son, our Lord."

We thank Thee that war with all its cruel desolations has ceased in our land. We pray that peace may henceforth abide with us and all the nations of the world. Give rulers and statesmen wisdom to know how best, in a world of sin and selfishness, to hasten the time when nations shall learn war no more; show them that there is a more excellent way than by bloodshed of securing the triumph of right, justice and patriotism among themselves. We ask Thine especial blessing upon our State and upon all our sister States of the South who were loyal to the Cause represented by that pure patriot and spotless statesman, Jefferson Davis, their first and only President.

May Thy blessing rest upon our whole country, North and South, upon our children and our children's children, and ever grant that a noble lesson be taught them of unselfish devotion to duty and splendid valor whenever they look upon this monument erected in loving memory of one whose devotion to his country was an inspiration to his soldiers, no less when the tide of battle was running fiercest against them, than in the laxity and monotony of camp.

Grant that those whose privilege it was to serve under this peerless cavalry General, may never lose sight of the humble and devout Christian in the dazzling glory of the military hero, and that while they can never forget his glad and wondrously cheerful devotion to duty amid the confused noise and roar of battle, amid bursting shells and countless death-dealing missiles, may they and their children still more firmly cherish the remembrance of his purity of life, his temperance and childlike faith in God his Savior, and that he lived among his most intimate friends such a life as in all the subsequent years to make virtue seem altogether loveable to them, and goodness wholly attractive. May they often recall that on an afternoon in the month of May, having battled gloriously for his beloved country near this city, and having successfully defended it, he sheathed his sword in the hour of victory and bowed his head in submission to God's will and then went to heaven.

In Thy sore chastisement of the South, when four years of war issued at last in defeat, we cherish the belief that Thou didst often temper judgment with mercy and loving kindness unto us and that the whole world was made to see that "Thou hadst a favour" unto us. And in order that those who finally triumphed should not be too much swollen with pride and say "my power and the might of mine hand hath done" these things, it seemed good to Thee in the accomplishment of Thy far-reaching purposes, that they should find it necessary — alas, for the awful sacrifice of human life — to recruit their shattered armies year after year from almost every nation under heaven. And then in our defeat — hardest of all to bear. because it was felt that Thou alone didst it — divine comfort was ministered to the vanquished by the heart-sustaining belief that Thou couldst yet say to them, "Well done good and faithful servants, what I do ye know not now, but ye shall know hereafter."

Help us and our children, O Lord, faithfully to cherish in a world of sordid selfishness and cunning policy, not only the examples of our consecrated leaders but also of their matchless followers the faithful private soldiers of the Southern Confederacy, who forsaking the velvet lawns of home and ease, gladly trod with bared bosom and bleeding feet the rugged stony path of duty, "taking no gain of money," scorning danger and courting death. And then, tho' with a bitter struggle of faith and many a tear — pardon, Lord, their momentary doubts — the maimed and ragged remnant furled with sacramental reverence the proud banner that oft had heard their prayers in camp and by bivouac fire and shouts of victory on full many a hard-contested battle field.

We thank Thee, O Lord, for all the blessings of established peace, and that those who for a time were estranged and contended fiercely with prodigal valor for the mastery in settling questions which were part of the heritage of our whole country, are living now in harmony and friendship, having a fresh conviction of the truth that "God is no respecter of persons, but in every nation he that feareth him and worketh righteousness is accepted with Him." We rejoice in believing that, through that severe ordeal of war, both sides have been prepared for greater achievements than could otherwise have been attained, and we pray that whatever in the future Thy providence may open before us in the march of human history, our only contention may be who shall first recognize

Thy beckoning hand and be foremost in doing Thy will. May we all lay well to heart that, as "the Captain of our Salvation was made perfect through suffering," so the nation, or the individual who best can bear the blows of outrageous fortune in the path of duty — "baptized with the baptism of blood" — will eventually accomplish most and be honored most by Thee as Thy chosen servants.

Lord, forgive, if at this time, or during the coming years, any old battle-scarred veterans beholding this life-like effigy — a flood of memories overwhelming them — should forget for the moment, all the blessings of peace, and all the Gospel's sweet teachings of love and forgiveness, and suddenly wish once again to be riding in columns of four with their beloved General (hearing his clarion voice above the din of battle) leading a charge as a thunderbolt from heaven with his squadrons, regiments and brigades following, rushing with one mighty impulse against the enemy "whose horse hoofs are broken, by means of their prancings, the prancings of their mighty ones," and then returning hear him again as of old "give his God and his father's God thanks, who teacheth him to war and girdeth him with strength of battle."

O Thou, who "canst be touched with a feeling of man's infirmities," forgive their foolish momentary wish, and fill their minds with better desires. Yet God forbid that we should be such unworthy followers of our immortal leaders that our lives should be spent in dwelling exclusively, or unduly, upon the great deeds and feats of war accomplished in a glorious past, content that our hopes and aspirations be buried in the grave of a Lost Cause, but graciously grant that we may be ever ready to follow as of old, with swift feet and indomitable resolution, the shifting field of battle of right against wrong, wherever Thy providence may call and Thy beckoning hand point us, and reckon, that perfect loyalty to the past does not require apathy as regards new questions and new issues, rather may the glorious past prove an unfailing fountain of inspiration, begetting unswerving fidelity to duty, caring less at any time for immediate success than that we may be found always battling against any odds for the right, as it is given us to see it.

O Lord Jesus Christ, who art the great "Captain of our Salvation," we thank Thee in Thy Holy Word it is recorded that Thou didst receive acceptable service from soldiers, and that Thou didst honor one with the exalted position of being the first person from the vast Gentile world to be admitted into union with Thy Kingdom on earth. And that it was the privilege of another soldier, when all of Thine own disciples had forsaken Thee as Thou didst hang upon the cruel Cross and all seemed lost, to declare in that darkest hour "truly this was a Son of God." And that of another brother soldier whose meek humility esteemed it too great an honor that Thou should come under his roof, that Thou didst say of him "I have not found so great faith, no not in Israel."

Grant, Lord, that every true and faithful soldier may still be dear to Thee, and now that the old Grey line is fast growing thinner, month by month and week by week, look with tenderest compassion upon them, be Thou their strength and shield. And as each one with bending form and weary feet approaches the Heavenly Home of many mansions, having lost all, it may be, save honor and integrity and love of the brethren and humble dutifulness to Thee, meet him, blessed Lord, with Thy forgiving love, Thy sustaining grace, and Thine approving smile, support him across the river, to rest with Thee and Thy redeemed ones under the shade of the trees, till, refreshed, he shall then again be ready, if it be Thy will, to serve Thee with a glad and willing service in the armies of heaven, through the unending ages of eternity.

— *Walter Quarrier Hullihen, 1907*

IMMIGRATION

A Prayer for Immigrants

Thou great Champion of the outcast and the weak, we remember before thee the people of other nations who are coming to our land, seeking bread, a home, and a future. May we look with thy compassion upon those who have been drained and stunted by the poverty and oppression of centuries, and whose minds have been warped by superstition or seared by the dumb agony of revolt. We bless thee for all that America has meant to the alien folk that have crossed the sea in the past, and for all the patient strength and Godfearing courage with which they have enriched our nation. We rejoice in the millions whose life has expanded in the wealth and liberty of our country, and whose children have grown to fairer stature and larger thoughts; for we, too, are the children of immigrants, who came with anxious hearts and halting feet on the westward path of hope.

We beseech thee that our republic may no longer fail their trust. We mourn for the dark sins of past and present, wherein men who are held in honor among us made spoil of the ignorance and helplessness of the strangers and sent them to an early death. In a nation dedicated to liberty may they not find the old oppression and a fiercer greed. May they never find that the arm of the law is but the arm of the strong. Help our whole people henceforth to keep in leash the cunning that would devour the simple. May they feel here the pure air of freedom and face the morning radiance of a joyous hope.

For all the oppressed afar off who sigh for liberty; for all lovers of the people who strive to break their shackles; for all who dare to believe in democracy and the Kingdom of

God, make thou our great commonwealth once more a sure beacon-light of hope and a guide on the path which leads to the perfect union of law and liberty.

— *Walter Rauschenbusch, 1910*

Prayer for Immigrants (modern version)

Defender of the downtrodden, we remember before you the people of other nations who come to this country in search of opportunity and in flight from oppression. May we look on those whose lives have been stunted and limited by the poverty and injustice of the past and seared by the conflict and turmoil that afflict their native lands.

We bless you for all that America has meant to those who have come here by land or sea and for all the courage and strength and energy with which they have enriched this country. We rejoice in all those millions whose lives have been enriched by the wealth and freedom of this country and whose children have taken their own place among us, for many of us are the children of immigrants who came with mingled hopes and fears to this new place.

We ask forgiveness for the hostility with which the new-comers among us have so often been greeted and the exploitation which has too frequently been their lot. In this nation dedicated to liberty, may we learn to restrain the greed and self-seeking that are too common among us and work harder to ensure impartial administration of our laws. May new-comers find this land to be indeed a place of freedom where energy is rewarded and hopes and dreams are fulfilled.

May those in countries where freedom and opportunity are still limited by the powerful and destroyed by conflict, who yet dare to believe in democracy and the reign of God, see in our nation once more a beacon of hope and a witness to the fulfillment human beings can find where laws are designed for the common good and government officials seek the welfare of those they serve. — *Christopher Webber*

THE INDUSTRIAL REVOLUTION

For Employers

We invoke thy grace and wisdom, O Lord, upon all men of good will who employ and control the labor of men. Amid the numberless irritations and anxieties of their position, help them to keep a quiet and patient temper, and to rule firmly and wisely, without harshness and anger. Since they hold power over the bread, the safety, and the hopes of the workers, may they wield their powers justly and with love, as older brothers and leaders in the great fellowship of labor. Suffer not the heavenly light of compassion for the weak and the old to be quenched in their hearts. When they are tempted to follow the ruthless ways of others, and to sacrifice human health and life for profit, do thou strengthen their will in the hour of need, and bring to naught the counsels of the heartless. Save them from repressing their workers into sullen submission and helpless fear. May they not sin against the Christ by using the bodies and souls of men as mere tools to make things, forgetting the human hearts and longings of these our brothers.

Raise up among us employers who shall be makers of men as well as of goods. Give us masters of industry who will use their higher ability and knowledge in lifting the workers to increasing independence and vigor, and who will train their helpers for the larger responsibilities of the coming age. Give us men of faith who will see beyond the strife of the present and catch a vision of a nobler organization of our work, when all will still follow the leadership of the ablest, not in fear but by the glad will of all, and when none shall be master and none shall be man, but all shall stand side by side in a strong and righteous brotherhood of work.

— Walter Rauschenbusch, 1910

For Child Laborers

Thou great Father of the weak, lay thy hand tenderly on all the little children on earth and bless them. Bless our own children, who are life of our life, and who have become the heart of our heart. Bless every little child-friend that has leaned against our knee and refreshed our soul by its smiling trustfulness. Be good to all children who long in vain for human love, or for flowers and water, and the sweet breast of Nature. But bless with a sevenfold blessing the young lives whose slender shoulders are already bowed beneath the yoke of toil, and whose glad growth is being stunted forever. Suffer not their little bodies to be utterly sapped, and their minds to be given over to stupidity and the vices of an empty soul. We have all jointly deserved the millstone of thy wrath for making these little ones to stumble and fall. Grant all employers of labor stout hearts to refuse enrichment at such a price. Grant to all the citizens and officers of states which now permit this wrong the grace of holy anger. Help us to realize that every child of our nation is in very truth our child, a member of our great family. By the Holy Child that nestled in Mary's bosom; by the memories of our own childhood joys and sorrows; by the sacred possibilities that slumber in every child, we beseech thee to save us from killing the sweetness of young life by the greed of gain.   *— Walter Rauschenbusch, 1910*

For the Children of the Street

Heavenly Father, whose unveiled face the angels of little children do always behold, look with love and pity, we beseech thee, upon the children of the streets. Where men, in their busy and careless lives, have made a highway, these children of thine have made a home and a school, and are learning the bad lessons of our selfishness and our folly. Save them, and save us, O Lord. Save them from ignorance and brutality, from the shamelessness of lust, the hardness of greed, and the besotting of drink; and save us from the greater guilt of those that offend thy little ones, and from the hypocrisy of those that say they see and see not, whose sin remaineth. Make clear to those of older years the inalienable right of childhood to play, and give to those who govern our cities the will and ability to provide the places for play; make clear to those who minister to the appetite for recreation the guilt of them that lead astray thy children, and give them wisdom resolutely to put aside the two-edged sword of violence that turns on those who seize it. Raise up for them still more leaders of able mind and large heart, and give them grace to follow the wiser counsel. When they strive for leisure and health and a better wage, do thou grant their cause success, but teach them not to waste their gain on fleeting passions, but to use it in building fairer homes and a nobler manhood. Grant all classes of our nation a larger comprehension for the aspirations of labor and for the courage and worth of these our brothers, that we may cheer them in their struggles and understand them even in their sins. And may the upward climb of Labor, its defeats and its victories, in the farther reaches bless all classes of our nation, and build up for the republic of the future a great body of workers, strong of limb, clear of mind, fair in temper, glad to labor, conscious of their worth, and striving together for the final brotherhood of all men.

— *Walter Rauschenbusch, 1910*

THE SPANISH AMERICAN WAR

The Nation's Prayer

Judge of the earth, to whom
    The secret things are known,
Lo, in this hour of gloom
We come before thy throne.
The knees of Freedom's sons are bent
    To none, O Lord, but Thee;
At Thy tribunal we present
    Our motive and our plea.

Thou knowest all the cause,
    The crime and insult both;
Long have we taken pause,
    And even now are loath
To strike a blow — yet Honor calls,
    Her summons we obey;
Fit mate were we for knaves and thralls
    Who still would urge delay.

Not for ourselves we try
    The final test of war:
A tortured people cry
    For succor from afar;
Before the bar of Liberty
    Stands tyranny arraigned;
The cup she mixed of misery
    Shall by herself be drained.

If with a hand unclean
  We wrongly draw the sword,
Let Justice intervene
  To make our cause abhorred.
We would not dim a history
  In honor clear begun;
We crave, O Lord, no victory
  That is not rightly won.
Let other nations sneer;
  Accountable alone
To thee, O Lord, we fear
  No censure save Thine own.
The powers of earth are in Thy sight
  A pageant and a dream;
Thou ever art of truth and right
  The Arbiter supreme.

The bugle calls us forth,
  The fateful guns are aimed;
O, may we prove our worth,
  Our honor keep unstained!
We lift the gage; the issue stands
  For innocence or guilt;
Our cause we place within Thy hands;
  Deal with us as thou wilt.

—*Edward McQueen Gray, April 22, 1898*

WORLD WAR I

A Prayer for Victory and Peace

Our Father in Heaven, the inspiration of every generous impulse, every high and noble aspiration, we thank Thee from our heart of hearts for the "Spirit of '76," which gave to us the immortal Declaration of Independence, which led on to victory and the formation of our Glorious Republic, which has not only been the wonder but the admiration of the world. We thank Thee for the day which will be celebrated with more than usual interest throughout the length and breadth of the land. The native born and the naturalized citizen will vie with each other in making it memorable.

For the first time in its history it will be celebrated by our sister nations, who are engaged with us in fighting for the same principles for which our forefathers fought, in a worldwide war for humanity, liberty, justice, and equal rights for all mankind.

May it furnish new inspiration to us and our allies, which will bring victory to their arms; then an everlasting peace; to the glory and honor of Thy Holy Name. Amen.

— Henry N. Couden, July 1918

Former Enemies

Lord, there is not one that doeth good, no not one. We therefore approach Thee with a sense of guilt in that however much we may think we have been wronged, we too have wronged others. However much we have to forgive we also have much to be forgiven. We pray Thee first to rid us of our own national arrogance, our race pride, our selfish insularity which have made for strife and enmity in days past. Forgive our own nation, Lord, for the sins we have committed against international goodwill. Lord, we would forgive as we are forgiven. Let Thy love and compassion encompass those against whom we fought in the Great War. Heal their wounds; assuage their sufferings; right their wrongs. Unite us anew in the family of nations as companions in a common cause. For hatred give goodwill; for suspicion give trust; for aloofness give neighborliness, that we may together create that brotherhood ordained by Thee for mankind, through Him who is our great elder brother, Jesus Christ our Lord.

—*Charles Henry Brent, 1929*

WORLD WAR II

The Attack on Pearl Harbor, December 7, 1941

The attack on Pearl Harbor, December 7, 1941, took place on a Sunday. The Congress convened the next day to hear President Roosevelt refer to the previous date as "a day that will live in infamy" and to declare war on Japan. At the opening of the session, Senate Chaplain Ze Barney T. Phillips, D.D., Chaplain of the Senate, offered the following prayer:

O Thou blessed Christ, Companion of our days, Mediator of the Infinite God and the Creator of a new world of being which men may know if they follow Thee and in which Thy tender love is ever available to lonely and despairing souls: Help us to find in Thee a sustaining sense of justice which shall become a passion for the amelioration of the wrongs of men, as honor calls us to the defense of every sacred ideal of our beloved country.

Keep us fine and true in our individual and corporate lives, steadfast in purpose that we may endure with patience and calm determination every trial, discipline, and sacrifice through which we may be called upon to pass, as we meet the exactions of these days out of which must emerge the future destiny of mankind.

Bless Thou the Congress with intuition and courage; strengthen our President with the strength of Thine own indwelling, and comfort him with the knowledge that today the loyalty of every citizen is pledged under his leadership to the service of the Nation as it undertakes its solemn task.

Do Thou have in Thy holy keeping those who have given their lives in the service of our country, and grant that in the new life they may serve Thee with clearer vision and greater joy. Assuage the anguish of those who are thus bereft, be Thou their Comforter and Friend, and bring them to a fuller knowledge of Thy love.

> O Christ! Whose voice the waters heard
> And hushed their raging at Thy word,
> Who walked'st on the foaming deep,
> And calm amidst its rage didst sleep,
> Oh hear us when we cry to Thee,
> For those in peril on the sea! Amen.
> — *Ze Barney T. Phillips, 1941*

The D-Day Invasion, June 6, 1944

Almighty God: Our sons, pride of our nation, this day have set upon a mighty endeavor, a struggle to preserve our Republic, our religion and our civilization, and to set free a suffering humanity.

Lead them straight and true; give strength to their arms, stoutness to their hearts, steadfastness in their faith.

They will need Thy blessings. Their road will be long and hard. For the enemy is strong. He may hurl back our forces. Success may not come with rushing speed, but we shall return again and again; and we know that by Thy grace, and by the righteousness of our cause, our sons will triumph.

They will be sore tried, by night and by day, without rest — until the victory is won. The darkness will be rent by noise and flame. Men's souls will be shaken with the violences of war.

For these men are lately drawn from the ways of peace. They fight not for the lust of conquest. They fight to end conquest. They fight to liberate. They fight to let justice arise, and tolerance and good-will among all Thy people. They yearn but for the end of battle, for their return to the haven of home.

Some will never return. Embrace these, Father, and receive them, Thy heroic servants, into Thy kingdom.

With Thy blessing, we shall prevail over the unholy forces of our enemy. Help us to conquer the apostles of greed and racial arrogances. Lead us to the saving of our country, and with our sister nations into a world unity that will spell a sure peace — a peace invulnerable to the schemings of unworthy men. And a peace that will let all men live in freedom, reaping the just rewards of their honest toil.

Thy will be done, Almighty God. Amen.

— *Franklin D. Roosevelt, 1944*

Hiroshima, August 6, 1945

What was Hiroshima like, Jesus, when the bomb fell?

What went through the minds of mothers, what happened to the lives of children, what stabbed at the hearts of men when they were caught up in a sea of flame?

What was Auschwitz like, Jesus, when the crematoriums belched the stinking smoke from the burned bodies of people? When families were separated, the weak perished, the strong faced inhuman tortures of the spirit and the body. What was the concentration camp like, Jesus?

Tell us, Christ, that we, living now, are capable of the same cruelty, the same horror, if we turn our back on you, our brother, and our sisters and brothers. Save us from ourselves; spare us the evil of our hearts' good intentions, unbridled and mad. Turn us from our perversions of love, especially when these are perpetrated in your name. Speak to us about war, and about peace, and about the possibilities for both in our very human hearts.   — *Malcolm Boyd, 1965*

V-J Day

The end of the Second World War came in two installments: Victory in Europe, or V-E Day (May 8, 1945), and Victory over Japan, or V-J Day (August 15, 1945), the latter marking the end of the first (and so far only) truly world-wide war.

Merciful God and Universal Father:

With hearts overflowing in gratitude have we come to Thy sanctuary on this solemn day. We are jubilant, for the guns have ceased firing and the cannons have terminated their rolling thunder. We are thankful that the catastrophic and calamitous plague of battle and bloodshed has ended; that America's valiant armies of liberation have broken the lash of the Japanese and European oppressors; that peace has come, at last, to all Thy children. After trying years of war and destruction, enslaved nations on all continents have been set free.

We shall always remember with humility and gratitude the dedicated and courageous men and women of our land whose patriotic devotion and supreme sacrifices enabled us to see victory and peace. We shall ever be grateful for the selfless and determined leaders who, imbued with unflinching faith in Thee and the cause of liberty, consecrated their energies to preserve the Four Freedoms for mankind.

Help us to refashion our world in a spirit of justice, and to lay the foundations of a universal society in which all Thy children will realize that we all have but One Father, and that Thou dist create us all, a world in which all nations and all men will be united in the bonds of brotherhood before Thee. Amen. — *Louis Swichkow, 1945*

THE COLD WAR AND AFTERWARD

A Prayer for Peace

Almighty and merciful God, Father of all men, creator and ruler of the universe, lord of history, whose designs are inscrutable, whose glory is without blemish, whose compassion for the errors of men is inexhaustible, in Your will is our peace.

Mercifully hear this prayer which rises to You from the tumult and desperation of a world in which You are forgotten, in which Your name is not invoked, Your laws are derided and Your presence is ignored; because we do not know You, we have no peace.

From the heart of an eternal silence, You have watched the rise of empires and have seen the smoke of their downfall.

You have seen Egypt, Assyria, Babylon, Greece, and Rome, once powerful, carried away like sand in the wind.

You have witnessed the impious fury of ten thousand fratricidal wars, in which great powers have torn whole continents to shreds in the name of peace and justice.

And now our Nation itself stands in imminent danger of a war the like of which has never been seen.

This Nation dedicated to freedom, not to power, has obtained through freedom a power it did not desire.

And seeking by that power to defend its freedom, it is enslaved by the processes and policies of power. Must we wage a war we do not desire, a war that can do us no good, and which our very hatred of war forces us to prepare?

A day of ominous decision has now dawned on this free Nation. Armed with a titanic weapon and convinced of our own right, we face a powerful adversary, armed with the same weapon, equally convinced that he is right.

In this moment of destiny, this moment we never foresaw, we cannot afford to fail. Our choice of peace or war may decide our judgment and publish it in an eternal record.

In this fatal moment of choice in which we might still begin the patient architecture of peace, we may also take the last step across the rim of chaos.

Save us then from our obsessions. Open our eyes, dissipate our confusions, teach us to understand ourselves and our adversary. Let us never forget that sins against the law of love are punished by loss of faith, and those without faith stop at no crime to achieve their ends.

Help us to be masters of the weapons that threaten to master us. Help us to use our science for peace and plenty, not for war and destruction. Show us how to use atomic power to bless our children's children, not to blight them.

Save us from the compulsion to follow our adversaries in all that we most hate, confirming them in their hatred and suspicion of us.

Resolve our inner contradictions, which now grow beyond belief and beyond bearing; they are at once a torment and a blessing, for if You had not left us the light of conscience, we would not have to endure them.

Teach us to be long-suffering in anguish and insecurity. Teach us to wait and trust. Grant light, grant strength and patience to all who work for peace — to this Congress, our President, our military forces, and our adversaries. Grant us prudence in proportion to our power, wisdom in proportion to our science, humaneness in proportion to our wealth and might. And bless our earnest will to help all races and peoples to travel, in friendship with us, along the road to justice, liberty and lasting peace.

But grant us above all to see that our ways are not necessarily Your ways, that we cannot fully penetrate the mystery of Your designs, and that the very storm of power now raging on this earth reveals Your hidden will and Your inscrutable decisions.

Grant us to see Your face in the lightening of this cosmic storm, O God of holiness, merciful to men, grant us to seek peace where it is truly found.

In Your will, O God, is our peace. Amen

— *Thomas Merton, Holy Week 1962*

The Assassination of John F. Kennedy, November 22, 1963

Almighty God, Omnipotent Author of Life:

With grief-stricken hearts and sorrowful spirits are we assembled on this National Day of Mourning to lament the untimely and tragic passing of a great humanitarian and illustrious leader of men.

Our heads are bowed in grief as we realize that John Fitzgerald Kennedy, 35th President of the United States, commander in chief of the armed forces of our country and chief executive of the world's arsenal of democracy, has been removed from our midst by the assassin's bullets. The sudden and shocking death of our President has resounded through-out the nation and the whole civilized world as a painful and catastrophic blow. To Americans of all creeds and races, his untimely departure from our midst at a crucial period in the annals of civilization leaves an empty space in the ranks of our nation and in the councils of the world.

By Thy grace, O Supreme King of Kings, and through the democratic choice of the American people, John Fitzgerald Kennedy was chosen to serve as the High Priest of "the land of the free." His vigorous, dynamic, courageous, and forthright character endeared him in the hearts of free people the world over. Fearlessly and unflinchingly he denounced the sinister forces of greed and bigotry. Inspired by the prophets of old, he championed the cause of human dignity and fought for the inalienable rights of all men, regardless of race or creed. Valiantly and courageously he took up the banner of justice and freedom. To all nations who cherished peace, he offered a warm, cordial handclasp of brotherhood.

We pray Thee, grant consolation to his bereaved family and the sorrowing citizenry of our land. May the name John Fitzgerald Kennedy ever be reverently linked with America's and mankind's immortals. Amen.

> — *Louis J. Swichkow, the National Day of Mourning,*
> *November 25, 1963*

The Vietnam War

At Yale University, May 5, 1972

Almighty God our heavenly Father, we ask thy blessing upon our nation as we enter the new agony and danger of heavier warfare. Watch over the people of Vietnam in the unimaginable suffering to which they are exposed. Grant our leaders the wisdom and humility to seek a peaceful solution and an end to aggression. Fill the hearts of our own people with the perseverance to continue unabated the work for peace. And grant thy blessing to [us] as we face the hard decisions of these days, that from the austerity we face, a spirit of unity and courage may arise to carry us forward with even greater dedication to the cause of learning and of truth.

— *Paul Moore Jr. 1972*

After Watergate, 1972–1974

Take from us, O God, all moral cowardice, every inclination to get along by going along.

Confirm in us your spirit of integrity, that when we know what is right we may do it. Give us confidence that truth will prevail, so we may be loyal to truth and thus to you who are the Truth.

Grant that what we ask others to do, we may do ourselves, so that righteousness and peace may dwell in our land and the joy of the Lord be our strength under God. Amen.

— *John B. Coburn, 1975*

A Prayer after the Oklahoma City Bombing, April 19, 1995

I am the building that was blown apart by a bomb in the "heartland" of America. My heart is blown open. The front of me falls away: I am the gaping floors, the broken glass, the dangling wires, the film of concrete dust that rises into the air.

This is my body.

I am the children who were killed: the little ones, the innocent, tender little people full of play and laughter. The babies.

This is my body.

I am the women and men who were killed, the mother, father, husband, wife, grandparent, neighbor, relative, friend, startled by death on an ordinary day.

This is my body.

I am those who mourn: the suddenly bereaved, the shocked, the bereft. I am the mother clutching a picture of her two children, the husband grieving his newlywed wife.

This is my body.

I am the rescue workers, the medical personnel, those who hope against hope, and those who are faithful even when there is no hope, those who press on into the rubble, searching for the living, the wounded, the dead, searching for what is human, for what is loved.

This is my body.

I am the ones who planned and planted the bomb: the hard-hearted, the fearful, the numb and angry ones who no longer care.

This is my body.

I am the ones who fill the airwaves with venom and hate. "Take them out in the desert and blow them up." "Shoot 'em." "I hope they fry."

This is my body.

I am the Holy Spirit, brooding over our bent world with bright wings. I am the wings of Jesus, tenderly outstretched above the city, sheltering everything and everyone beneath.

This is my body.

I cannot hold it all. I hand it to you, Jesus. Hold it with me. And suddenly I see that I am handing you the cross: here, you carry it. I cannot.

And he has taken it up. He is carrying all of this, all of this. The dead, the wounded, and those who mourn; the killers and those who were killed; the frightened, the angry, the sorrow-ful — he is carrying all of this, all of us, every part of us, into the loving heart of God.   — *Margaret Bullitt-Jonas, 1995*

The Clinton Impeachment Proceedings, January 7, 1999

"Is there any word from the Lord?"

We humbly fall on the knees of our hearts as this ancient, urgent biblical question reverberates in our minds and echoes in this historic Chamber. When there is nowhere else to turn, we return to You, dear God. We hear Your answer sound-ing in our souls: "Let him who glories glory in this, that he understands and knows Me, that I am the Lord, exer-cising loving kindness, judgment, and righteousness in the earth." — Jeremiah 9:24. Your righteous judgment is irre-ducible and Your grace irrefutable. Holy God, as this sacred Chamber becomes a court and these Senators become ju-rors, be omnipresent in the pressures of these impeachment proceedings.

Grant the Senators the ability to exercise clear judgment without judgmentalism. Today, unite the Senate in nonparti-san commitment to the procedures that will most effectively resolve the grave matters before them and our Nation. Bind the Senators together as fellow patriots seeking Your best for our beloved land.

Oh, dear Father, author of this Republic and divine authority from whom the Senators' powers flow, we trust You. With one mind and heart, we rededicate ourselves to You and thank You for Your guidance each step of the way through these troubled times. You are our Lord and Savior. Amen.

— *Senate Chaplain, Lloyd John Ogilvie, 1999*

The 9/11 Attack, September 11, 2001

Almighty God, source of strength and hope in the darkest hours of our Nation's history, we praise You for the consistency and constancy of Your presence with us to help us confront and battle the forces of evil manifested in infamous, illusive, cowardly acts of terrorism. We turn to You with hearts filled with dismay, anger, and grief over the terrorist attacks on the World Trade buildings in New York City and the Pentagon here in Washington. We pray for the thousands of victims who lost their lives as a result of these violent acts against our Nation. We intercede for their loved ones; comfort them and give them courage. In particular, we pray for the loved ones of the fire fighters and police who died seeking to help others. Quiet our turbulent hearts. Remind us of how You have been with us in trouble and tragedies of the past and have given us victory over tyranny. Bless the women and men of this Senate today as they join with President Bush in decisive action. Guide them as they seek justice against the perpetrators of yesterday's evil destruction and seek to devise a long-range solution to the insidious problem of terrorism. Thank You in advance for the courageous leadership You will provide through this Senate. You are our Lord and Savior. Amen.

— *Senate Chaplain, Lloyd John Ogilvie, on September 12, 2001*

Remembering September 11, 2001

A prayer to be used in observances of the anniversary of September 11, 2001.

God the compassionate one, whose loving care extends to all the world, we remember this day your children of many nations and many faiths whose lives were cut short by the fierce flames of anger and hatred. Console those who continue to suffer and grieve, and give them comfort and hope as they look to the future. Out of what we have endured, give us the grace to examine our relationships with those who perceive us as the enemy, and show our leaders the way to use our power to serve the good of all for the healing of the nations. This we ask through Jesus Christ our Lord who, in reconciling love, was lifted up from the earth that he might draw all things to himself. Amen.   — *Frank T. Griswold, 2001*

The Second Gulf War, 2003

On March 18, 2003, a coalition of forces led by the United States invaded Iraq to overthrow the regime of Saddam Hussein. The following prayers were offered in the next few days by guest Chaplains in the United States Congress.

God, whose aggression is born of love and whose aim is
       peace,
God of revelation and inspiration,
from Your Holy Word come instructions about the necessity
       of vision
and statements of encouragement for the entertainment of
       vision.
Help us, O God.
Our world needs a new vision of sovereignty.

We need negotiations more than confrontation,
   cooperation more than conflict,
   peace rather than war.
Help us, Lord.
Our world needs a new vision of freedom.
We need no political hostages; free them, Lord.
We need no slaves of prejudice; free them Lord.
No bond servants of poverty; free them, Lord.
No captives of hunger; free them, Lord.
No servants of sin; free them, Lord.
Our world needs a new vision of Your redemption.
Save us, Lord.
Enable us to call on Your name in repentance,
   to open our hearts to You in commitment,
   and to bow our knees to You in obedience.
Our prayer is offered in the Name of the One
   who gives clear visibility and spiritual reality. Amen.
       — *Willie Davis, House of Representatives Guest Chaplain*

Eternal God, we come before Thee in dangerous times. Many are anxious and fearful as the lives of our Nation's forces and their allies are in harm's way, opposing an evil and oppressive regime. We pray for swift victory and a safe return. We know that the one certainty of war is sacrifice. And yet there is the haunting thought that if nothing is worth fighting and dying for, then evil goes unchallenged, cruelty unthwarted, and oppression unchecked. What then is worth living for?

We pray for courage and inner strength for those young men and women, who, on their country's behalf, offer a forceful, yet vulnerable presence to compel a malevolent dictator's overthrow. Lord, we live in a day when the foundations of truth and goodness have been despised and denigrated and lives are built on hedonism, cynicism, and relativism. Yet these are sand, and after life's quaking storms only the things which cannot be shaken remain.

O God, let good be brought out of evil as people realize that freedom is a luxury, denied for most of history to most of humanity. Thus, may our gratitude for our own freedom be shown by never taking it for granted or using it wantonly, forgetting its cost in sacrifice, past and present.

May these Senators, as guardians of this precious freedom, be its sharers with others, as blessed by Thee. And may they use their position of power for a lasting purpose that benefits this fair land and far beyond. Amen.

— *Campbell Gillon, Guest Chaplain in the United States Senate*

Muslim Prayer for Peace in Iraq and Throughout the World

O God of Abraham, Moses, Jesus, and Muhammad! Bring peace and tranquility to the people of Iraq who have been plagued with pain and suffering;

O God! We appeal to You bring our soldiers back safe and help our nation to be one that is given to truth and justice.

O God! We call You with your beautiful names: the One, the Holy, the Sovereign, the Just, and the Peace. We call with love and sincerity to bring peace to our world and guide our steps to do what is right and what pleases You.

O God! You are the Source of Good, the Guardian of Faith, the Preserver of Safety, the Exalted in Might, the Supreme: All Glory belongs to You! Help us to see our glory in serving You and upholding the values of compassion and justice on earth.

O God we beg You to forgive our sins and ask You not to
        hold us accountable for mistakes and missteps we
        did or were done in our names. Our Lord give us the
        humility to recognize our mistakes and limitations,
        and the strength and courage to choose right over
        wrong and justice over pride.

O the Eternal and Compassionate Lord! Fill our hearts with
        Your Love, and help us to love one another, and
        show compassion to Your servants throughout the
        world and Your creation.

O God! We ask You in submission and humility to allow
        wisdom to triumph over vanity, truth over falsehood,
        and love over hate.

Amen.   —*Sayyid M. Syeed, 2007*

For Peace

Eternal God, Creator of the universe, there is no God but
        You.

Great and wonderful are Your works, wondrous are your
        ways.

Thank You for the many splendoured variety of Your
        creation.

Thank You for the many ways we affirm Your presence and
        purpose,

and the freedom to do so.

Forgive our violation of Your creation.

Forgive our violence toward each other.

We stand in awe and gratitude for Your persistent love

for each and all of Your children:

Christian, Jew, Muslim,

as well as those with other faiths.

Grant to all and our leaders attributes of the strong;

mutual respect in words and deed,
restraint in the exercise of power, and
the will for peace with justice, for all.
Eternal God, Creator of the universe, there is no God but
        You. Amen.

> — *This prayer, composed by Christian, Jewish and Muslim clergy, was used during the First Gulf War in 1991.*

PART THREE

Prayers for National Occasions

PRESIDENTIAL INAUGURATIONS

Inauguration of Franklin D. Roosevelt, March 4, 1933

Eternal God and Heavenly Father, before whose face the generations rise and pass away, who through all the ages hast led Thy children with the fire and cloud; hearken to our prayer and turn the heart of every citizen of the Republic unto Thee in this fateful hour of our own and the world's great need. Bestow Thy choicest blessings upon these Thy servants, who under Thee have been called to be President and Vice-President of the United States. Give unto them the grace of true humility, the heart that knows no guile, the courage born of innocency of life, the gentle patience of the Christ, and, above all, the spirit of love that believes and hopes and endures, that they may be true leaders of Thy people.

Bless every Member of the Congress and all others in authority, that they may be a glorious company, the flower of men, to serve a model for this mighty world and to be the fair beginning of a time when, with every root of bitterness cast out, the good work of all shall be the goal of each. Let Thy blessing rest upon the retiring President, Vice-President, and Members of the Congress, to whom we pay our loving tribute. Bring the nations of the world, through an ever-increasing sense of fellowship, into one great family; hasten the time when war shall be no more, and may we never be content with any peace save that of Him who won His peace by making the world's His own, Jesus Christ our Lord. Amen.

— *Ze Barney Phillips, 1933*

Inauguration of Dwight D. Eisenhower, January 20, 1953

Almighty God, as we stand here at this moment my future associates in the executive branch of government join me in beseeching that Thou will make full and complete our dedication to the service of the people in this throng, and their fellow citizens everywhere.

Give us, we pray, the power to discern clearly right from wrong, and allow all our words and actions to be governed thereby, and by the laws of this land. Especially we pray that our concern shall be for all the people regardless of station, race, or calling.

May cooperation be permitted and be the mutual aim of those who, under the concepts of our Constitution, hold to differing political faiths; so that all may work for the good of our beloved country and Thy glory. Amen.

— Dwight D. Eisenhower, 1953

Inauguration of George H. W. Bush, January 20, 1989

Our Father and our God, Thou hast said, "Blessed is the nation whose God is the Lord." We recognize on this historic occasion that we are a nation under God. This faith in God is our foundation and our heritage. Thou hast warned us in the Holy Scriptures, "If the foundations be destroyed, what can the righteous do?" We confess that we are in danger of destroying some of those foundations, for at times our faith in Thee has faltered and we have chosen to go our own way rather than the way that Thou wouldst have us go, both as individuals and as a nation. Forgive us, we pray, as we turn to Thee in repentance and faith. Restore us to Thyself and create within us a desire to follow Thy will for all our lives. As George Washington reminded us in his farewell address, morality and faith are the pillars of our society. May we never forget that.

And now we come to a new era in our history. In Thy sovereignty Thou hast permitted George Bush to lead us at this momentous hour of our history for the next four years. As he today places his hand upon the Bible and solemnly swears before Thee to preserve, protect and defend the Constitution, give him the wisdom, integrity and courage to help this become a nation that is gentle and kind. Protect him from physical danger, and in the lonely moments of decision grant him Thy wisdom to know what is morally right and an uncompromising courage to do it. Give him a cool head and a warm heart. Give him a compassion for those in physical, moral and spiritual need. O God, we consecrate today George Herbert Walker Bush to the presidency of these United States.

— *Billy Graham, 1993*

Inauguration of William Clinton, January 20, 1993

Our God and our Father, we thank you for this historic occasion when we inaugurate our new President and Vice-President. We thank you for the moral and spiritual foundations which our forefathers gave us and which are rooted deeply in scripture. Those principles nourished and guided us as a nation in the past, but we cannot say that we are a righteous people. We've sinned against you. We've sown to the wind and are reaping the whirlwind of crime, drug abuse, racism, immorality, and social injustice. We need to repent of our sins and turn by faith to you.

And now, on this twentieth day of January, 1993, we commit to you President-elect Clinton and Vice-President-elect Gore, whom you have permitted to take leadership at this critical time in our nation's history. Help them always to see the office to which they've been elected as a sacred trust from you. We pray that you will bless their wives who will share so much of the responsibility and burdens. Make President-elect Clinton know that he is never really alone but that the eternal God can be his refuge and he can turn to you in every circumstance. Give him the wisdom you've promised to those who ask and the strength that you alone can give. We thank you for his predecessor President Bush and the dedication he gave to this office. Bless him as he and Mrs. Bush continue their dedicated service to our country in other spheres. We commit this inaugural ceremony to you and ask that the memory of this event may always remind us to pray for our leaders. I pray this in the name of the one that's called Wonderful Counselor, Mighty God, the Everlasting Father and the Prince of Peace. Amen.   — *Billy Graham, 1993*

Martin Luther King Jr.

Martin Luther King Jr.'s Birthday, January 15, Observed on the Third Monday in January

Martin Luther King Jr. was an African American Baptist pastor who gained prominence through his leadership of a civil rights protest in Birmingham, Alabama, and became the chief spokesperson of the nonviolent civil rights movement. He was assassinated in 1968, and the federal holiday to honor his accomplishments was established in 1983. It was officially observed in all 50 states for the first time in 2000.

Memorial Prayer at Howard University in Memory of Martin Luther King Jr.

Eternal God, in the name of the Lord Jesus Christ, we would thank Thee today that Thou hast honored the purpose of our gathering. We thank Thee for sending unto us, this Nation, and the world our great departed leader, Dr. Martin Luther King Jr., the late possessor of unique gifts, dignity, graces, and eloquence of rare beauty. He was profoundly inspiring and challenging to his generation. The potency of his personality was marked by social progress, moral, and ethical reform.

Thou sent him to us as Thou sent Moses to Egypt to deliver the Hebrew people from slavery and bondage. We sincerely pray that the rich heritage of his philosophy may continue to inspire our Nation and Race to develop a social order of love, equality, brotherhood, compassion for black people, poor people, socially disinherited people, with dignity and justice for all people.

May the torch of non-violence which he held so high continue to burn brightly in spite of the great darkness that is covering our world today. May we never permit his dream to be an impossible dream. May we never surrender to the enemy which he fought so courageously, so bravely, and heroically to the end.

In his dwelling place among the immortals, grant that there be no future postponement, procrastination, and delay of the righteous demands that he made on the American establishment for a regeneration of our society.

> "Minorities since time began
> Have shown the better side of man,
> And often in the list of time
> One man has made a cause sublime."
> In His Name. Amen.
>
> —*Smallwood Edmond Williams, 1970*

We thank you, O God, that somehow in the midst of the confusion and disintegration of life you have spoken, as you often do, through one who was of the lineage and faith of an exploited people. So it is that at this time we remember Martin Luther King Jr., and as we do, we recall how strange it is that you often speak through those whom humankind has rejected. How strange — that from those who are the oppressed come the saviors not only of their own people but of all peoples everywhere. How profound and reassuring about the human spirit that those who are so markedly persecuted become the lovers of life, the peacemakers, and the instruments by which you establish human community and justice.

Martin King was a man who belonged to a race that has every reason to hate, and yet he preached by way of his actions an almost unbearable and seemingly ridiculous goodwill toward the enemy. When he spoke of creative goodwill — one that would suffer humiliation and ultimately change the heart of the oppressor — he dared risk the wrath, criticism, and disrespect of the society . . . and even his own people. But, Martin King believed with all his heart that you, God, the Creator of life, the Integrating Spirit that ties all life together, have revealed yourself in the flesh and blood of Jesus. And if one were going to walk the way that Jesus walked, one must be willing to take the road that leads to Calvary. Amen.

— George Thomas, 1983

Lord our God,
see how oppression and violence are our sad inheritance,
one generation to the next.
We look for you where the lowly are raised up,
where the mighty are brought down.
We find you there in your servants,

and we give you thanks this day for your preacher and
    witness,
Martin Luther King Jr.
Fill us with your spirit:
where our human community is divided by racism,
torn by repression,
saddened by fear and ignorance,
may we give ourselves to your work of healing.

Grant this through Christ our Lord. Amen.
        — *Catholic Household Blessings and Prayers, 1988*

O God of Love, Power and Justice, who wills the freedom of
all your children. We thank you for the constancy of your loving kindness and tender mercies toward us. Especially on this
day as we celebrate the birthday and life of your servant and
prophet, Dr. Martin Luther King Jr. We are reminded that in
every age you raise up seers and sayers and doers of justice.
We marvel at the way by which you shaped a young black boy
from Georgia into a towering figure of his time — to awaken
the conscience of the nations, to rekindle a passion for freedom, equality, and peace; to redirect the traffic of human
affairs from the back alley of bigotry toward the course of
courage and compassion. We stand in awe at the marvelous
networking by which you built a movement around a man of
vision. It included blacks and whites, Protestants, Catholics,
and Jews, conservatives and progressives, rich and poor, business and labor. This "coalition of conscience" dedicated itself
to the proposition that the American dream of freedom and
equality could be made real through courageous action in a
spirit of love, in pursuit of human dignity for all. This dignity includes all who suffer from homelessness, joblessness,
purposelessness, carelessness, hopelessness.

Because our needs are so great today, and your care so constant, we know that you are rebuilding the network of compassion around new visionaries who you have assembled for this hour. Surprise us with the discovery of how much power we have to make a difference in our day:

+ A difference in the way citizens meet, greet, respect, and protect the rights of each other.

+ A difference in the breadth of our vision of what is possible in humanization, reconciliation, and equalization of results in our great city.

+ A difference in the way government, business, and labor can work together, for justice and social enrichment.

+ A difference in our response to the needy, and a difference in appreciation for those who give of themselves for the surviving and thriving of our beautiful people.

Use this season of celebration to spark new hope and stir up our passion for new possibilities. Make compassion and the spirit of sacrifice to be the new mark of affluence of character. Strengthen us to face reality and to withstand the rigor of tough times in the anticipation of a bright side beyond the struggle. Inspire, empower, and sustain us until we reach the mountaintop, and see that future for which our hearts yearn.

This is our fervent and sincere prayer. Amen.

—*James Alexander Forbes Jr., 1990*

God of grace and glory, light and love, hear our prayer.

We offer thanks that you have drawn us together as your people, as a community of faith, as a family of individuals bound to one another through a common relationship with you. Be near to us in our doubts and trials. Encourage us beyond our pains and upsets. Renew us through our hopes and joys. Fill us with a deepening recognition of our ongoing need for spiritual direction and growth. Help us dare to share our faith with others, always being open to dialogue and accepting of diverse understandings. We have a variety of gifts to offer. By your grace, we can unwrap them and put them to good use.

We offer thanks that there is purpose in your drawing us together. You urge us beyond the limits of a private piety to be as salt to food and as light to darkness. You lead us to live out our faithfulness in ways that preserve and brighten the world. Charge us with devoted and Christly love that we might challenge the powers of injustice and confront the enemies of peace. We confess our own capacity to deny the dignity of others. We are guilty of using aggression to achieve our own goals. We ask that you enable us to rise above these failings to be pursuers of justice and makers of peace.

We offer special thanks today for one who showed the essential connection between a growing spirit and expanding commitment to justice and peace. We pray that the strength to love that was embodied in the life of Martin Luther King Jr., may inspire us to be stronger believers in the dream he dreamed and bolder enactors of the kind of faith he held. Help us to learn from his life a way of witness that can keep working to overcome what is wrong and to nurture what is right.

We offer our prayer in the name of Jesus Christ. Amen.

— *Glen E. Rainsley, 1991*

For an Inter-faith Commemoration of the Life of Martin Luther King Jr.

> Lord God of freedom,
> we give you thanks and praise
> because you have raised up men and women
> to lead your people to freedom;

we thank you for Moses and Miriam,
for Joshua and Deborah,
for Jael and Ezra and Nehemiah,
for Simon and Judas Maccabeus,
for George Washington and Abraham Lincoln,
for Harriet Tubman and Susan B. Anthony;
especially we give you thanks and praise
that in our day you raised up Martin Luther King Jr.
to hold before us the dream and the vision
of one people, united in justice and free at last
to use the gifts you have given them
in joy and thankfulness
for the benefit of all people
and to the glory of your Name.
For these witnesses, for this day,
for the dream by which we still are guided,
we give you thanks and praise,
O Lord our God. Amen.

— Christopher L. Webber, 1992

PRESIDENTIAL BIRTHDAYS

Americans began celebrating George Washington's birthday (February 22) while he was still in office but it was not made an official national holiday until 1885. Abraham Lincoln's birthday (February 12) was widely celebrated in northern states but has never been made a federal holiday. In 1968 the Congress attempted to rationalize the various national celebrations and decreed that the third Monday in February should be kept as Washington's Birthday. Some had wanted to make it "Presidents' Day" but although Congress rejected that proposal, the notion that it was adopted has become widespread and it is so marked on many calendars. The fact that the third Monday in February is always before Washington's actual birthday and after Lincoln's makes the inclusive title logical. There are, as a result of this confusion, few if any prayers for "Presidents' Day" as such and it has been necessary to compose one for this book.

George Washington's Birthday

The following prayer was composed by Archbishop John Carroll in the eighteenth century for Washington's birthday but was altered in 1988 to make it more generally useful.

Almighty and eternal God,
you have revealed your glory to all nations.
God of power and might, wisdom and justice,
through you authority is rightly administered,
laws are enacted, and judgment is decreed.
Assist with your spirit of counsel and fortitude
the President of these United States,
that his/her administration
   may be conducted in righteousness,
and be eminently useful to your people
   over whom he/she presides.
May he/she encourage due respect for virtue and religion.
May he/she execute the laws with justice and mercy.
May he/she seek to restrain crime, vice, and immorality.
We, likewise, commend to your unbounded mercy
all who dwell in the United States.
Bless us and all people with the peace which the world
      cannot give.
We pray to you, who are Lord and God, for ever and ever.
Amen.   — *Archbishop John Carroll (alt.), Catholic Household*
Blessings and Prayers, 1988

We thank Thee, our Father in heaven, that time has not diminished the admiration, gratitude, and reverence for the "Father of his Country"; that he still lives in the hearts of all true men, the ideal patriot, soldier, statesman, Christian gentleman. "Taking him for all in all, we shall not look upon his like again." Wise, strong, pure, noble, admiration of all peoples. We thank Thee that millions of hearts still beat in unison with his great heart, for so long as his influence shall thus live our Nation shall live and liberty widen its sweep among the peoples of the earth, to the honor and glory of Thy holy name. Amen.   — *Henry N. Couden, 1913*

God of Truth, Supreme Sovereign of the Universe:

In this month of February, we pause to honor the memory of an illustrious American, whose enduring contributions to the founding of our Republic have made him immortal — George Washington.

From Valley Forge, to that historic hour when he pronounced the solemn oath as the first President of the United States, George Washington dedicated his life to make the boon of freedom secure for future generations. On the field of battle and in the Sanctuary of the Republic, the Father of his Country fought and labored with all his heart for the land he loved. Under his leadership, thirteen colonies became a united nation, giving "to bigotry no sanction, to persecution no assistance"; a powerful Citadel of Democracy, an inspiration for liberty-loving nations the world over.

May the patriotism, wisdom, and courageous spirit of Washington motivate us and our fellow Americans to consecrate ourselves to preserve, at all costs, the precious freedom and sacred rights we enjoy. Gird us with strength to safeguard our American way of life, for which Washington and his fellow countrymen gave so much. Amen.

— *Louis J. Swichkow, 1964*

Abraham Lincoln's Birthday

O God, our Father, how great are Thy mysteries, how inscrutable are Thy ways, yet Thy holy influence touches the hearts of men and inspires to deeds of heroism and glory. The day of miracles will never end. Abraham Lincoln, born as lowly as the Savior of men, with little or no opportunity for an education and few books to guide him, increased in wisdom and knowledge and became the exponent of all that is purest and best. Surely he was the man of God, chosen to guide our ship of state through the terrible storm which broke upon it to a safe harbor, "with malice toward none and charity for all." He has builded for himself a monument more grand and imposing than the mind of man has yet conceived, which reaches from the earth beneath to the heavens above. Grant as the years come and go it may grow more stately, shine more brightly, a beacon light to guide us and future generations till the genius of our Republic shall be fulfilled in a union of brain and brawn and heart, to the glory and honor of Thy holy name. Amen.

— Henry N. Couden, 1912

We rejoice in the birthday of Abraham Lincoln, the spiritual center of our history. We pray thee to move us, the American people, closer to our center. Free us, O God, from the fear that corrupts our wisdom for the sake of power; from the fear that trivializes, that divides us as a people, especially rich from poor; from the fear that prompts us to make authority our truth instead of truth our authority. And we pray for the church, that it may be courageous and compassionate in times that are sure to be uncertain.

Guide, O most merciful Creator, the thinking of rulers the world around. May they not confuse violence with strength or compassion with weakness. May they not use the imperfections of international relations as an excuse to perpetuate them; rather, may they see that the high purpose of rulers is to keep hope advancing, to straighten out this tangled world, to make people good — by their own choosing.

With malice toward none and charity to all, may we all press forward until we can say of this world what we can gratefully say of this day, "Beautiful, beyond any singing of it." Amen.   — *William Sloane Coffin Jr., 1983*

Presidents' Day

This prayer is also suitable as a general prayer for the nation.

Eternal God, who hast made us so that our hearts are restless until they rest in thee, we make our approach to thee in hope and expectation. In this house of praise and prayer we have often heard thy voice and seen thy glory. Here we have found release from the tension of life. Here our fears and forebodings have vanished. Here the deepest cravings of our natures have been satisfied. Renew to us these mercies. Grant us now a vivid sense of thy nearness. Fill our hearts with joy and our lips with song.

Forgive us, we beseech thee, for our sins. We are not what we ought to be. We have done things which we ought not to have done; we have left undone things which we ought to have done; there are times when, despairingly, we wonder whether there is any health in us. Pardon our offenses, O God — our selfishness, our thoughtlessness, our persistent neglect of thee. So change our hearts and renew our wills, that we shall love that which thou dost love and do that which thou dost command, and with singleness of mind and purpose seek first thy kingdom and thy righteousness.

O gracious God, who hast cast our lot in pleasant places, we praise thee for our goodly heritage in this land. We remember with gratitude those whose gifts of head and heart and hand established the foundations of this nation. We bless thee for the ideals of faith and freedom which they cherished. Help us to hold them dear and to prize them above luxury or ease. Deliver us from pride and self-sufficiency. In prosperity, let us not forget thee; in the hour of achievement let us not be unmindful of our dependence on thee. Grant to our leaders purity of motive, soundness of judgment, the faith of their forebears, and to all our people fidelity, integrity, and real religion, that there may be peace and prosperity within our borders and that we may be an influence for righteousness throughout the world.

Raise up in every land leaders of vision and courage who for the sake of the common good will think wisely and do justly and love mercy. Let goodwill reign in the hearts of all humankind, and bring us speedily out of our present confusion into the order and righteousness of thy kingdom; through him who is the Prince of peace and the Savior of the world, in whose spirit and name we pray. Amen.

— Robert J. McCracken, 1983

Guide, Guardian, and Sustainer of our common life,
we give you thanks for all those
who have served as President of this country,
for the far-sighted wisdom and humility
of George Washington
in rejecting the titles and trappings of monarchy
to provide a model of leadership
subservient always to the laws
and seeking always the good of the citizens;
for the patient endurance and courage

of Abraham Lincoln in seeking national unity above all
and calling the country to reconciliation
with malice toward none; with charity for all;
with firmness in the right, as God gives us to see the right;
for all those who have come from so many of our states,
from so many different backgrounds and circumstances,
in times of prosperity and times of hardship,
in times of war and seasons of peace,
each, according to the gifts they were given,
serving in the great office to which they were elected.
Pour out, we pray, the spirit of wisdom and understanding
on (N.) who serves as president at this time,
and grant that (he/she) may always seek first your will
and put aside all the temptations of power and influence
to serve this people and seek peace with all people.
Grant that the great vision of equal justice under the law
may continue to inspire the President and all who hold office
and that they may turn always to prayer for your guidance
knowing that they must at last give account for all their
        actions
to you who have called us always
to seek your kingdom and your righteousness.
                              — *Christopher L. Webber, 2008*

MEMORIAL DAY

The Last Monday in May

*Memorial Day was initiated as a day to honor those who had
died in the Civil War. It was called "Decoration Day" and
was observed on May 30 because that was not the date of
any particular Civil War battle. After the First World War it*

was expanded to include those who had died in all American wars and as of 1971 was fixed on the last Monday in May.

Almighty God, our heavenly Father, in whose hands are the living and the dead; we give thee thanks for all those thy servants who have laid down their lives in the service of our country. Grant to them thy mercy and the light of thy presence, that the good work which thou hast begun in them may be perfected; through Jesus Christ our Lord. Amen.

— *Book of Common Prayer, 1928*

We bow our heads this day, O God, in memory of those who laid down their lives that others might live. They redeemed for us our liberties; they saved us from oppression and debasement; they pushed back barbarous evils that were threatening to engulf us; they gave us at fearful cost, the promise of tomorrow.

To them, as to us, the life of earth seemed fair and bright; they loved the blueness of the sky, the firmness of the ground beneath their feet, the snows of winter, the blossoming of spring. They loved the works of man, the busy world, the tasks before them. They loved their homes, their families, the companions they had chosen for life's journey, their intimates and friends.

But more than this they loved the virtue that mankind must live by: the truth that was being trampled and the vision that had been profaned. They loved their honor and their duty. And so they fought and died. Let not their lives be given in vain!

Let our hearts remember, O God of Mercy, the many who waited for them and who learned at last that they would not return. Let there be a stillness in us, a deepness of humility, when we remember the bereaved.

O God! That some should give so much! And others almost nothing! Stir us, arouse us, goad us on to new resolve! We have been willing to forget, we have served the trivial moment and not the opportunity they gave us. Turn us away, O God, from living in life's sheltered places. Deepen our soul's disquietude, our heart's unrest. Until we are willing for the claims upon us, made sacred by the sacrifice of those who died.

They gave us tomorrow! The tomorrow they themselves would not return to share. They left us bright dreams! Dreams that for them could not come true. Paid for in blood: the blood of youth with pulse and passion; and in the grief of the vainly waiting, who were told that those they loved would not come back. This was the cost: the cost unspeakable! O God, be with us! Make us worthy! Lift us up in high resolve!

When we remember, O God, those we have loved and lost, help us to remember also how great a thing is loving, and that not to have loved would have been far greater loss.

— *A. Powell Davies, 1956*

Almighty God, Father of all Mankind:

We pause on this Day of Memorial to honor the memories of the heroic sons of our country who rendered their full measure of devotion on all the far-flung battlefields of the world, in the defense of these United States.

They fought valiantly and courageously in storms of fire and blood, so that we, the living, may enjoy the blessings of liberty, democracy, and freedom.

May the deeds of our fallen heroes be an inspiration to us and to all our fellow Americans. Grant that their supreme sacrifices shall not have been in vain. Let this Memorial Day stimulate us to be mindful of our responsibilities and duties as conscientious citizens of this great Republic.

We pray Thee, Merciful Father, sustain the leaders of the United Nations in their efforts to remove the dark shadow of fear which lurks over the abodes of peace-loving peoples. Help all nations of our twentieth-century world to realize the cruelty of bloodshed and the futility of warfare. Inspire them to labor with all their might to banish conflict and strife, and to establish world peace.

Hasten the fulfillment of the visions of our Prophets when the work of righteousness shall be peace, and its effect, tranquility and security forever; when nation shall not lift up sword against nation, neither shall they learn war anymore. Amen. — *Louis J. Swichkow, 1964*

Lord God, in whom there is life and light:
Accept
our thanks for those who died for us,
our prayers for those who mourn,
our praise for the hope You have given us.
Refresh our hearts
with dedication to heroic ideals,
with appreciation for the honesty of the just,
with obedience to upright laws.
Forgive us
when our patriotism is hollow,
when our nationalism is arrogant,
when our allegiance is halfhearted.
Stir within us
thanksgiving for all we have inherited,
vigilance for the freedoms of all people,
willingness to sacrifice for fellow citizens.
Comfort us with the joy that Christ died
for all those who died for us,

bringing life and immortality to light
for all who believe in Him. Amen.
— *The Lutheran Book of Prayer, 1970, adapted*

Gracious God, whose own Son's term of service to humanity was so full that its brevity was no distress, we call to mind on this Memorial Sunday those "who will not grow old as we who are left grow old," those whose lives were too brief for us but long enough, perhaps, for thee. Forgive us that they died so young because we were too unimaginative, too imperious, too indifferent, or just too late to think of better ways than warfare to conduct the business of the world. Gratefully we remember the generosity that prompted them to share the last of their rations, the last pair of dry socks, to share in the course of one hour in a foxhole more than most of us care to share with another in a lifetime. And we recall the courage that made more than one of them fall on the grenade there was no time to throw back.

Grant, O God, that they may not have died in vain. May we draw new vigor from past tragedy. Buttress our instincts for peace, sorely beleaguered. Save us from justifications invented to make us look noble, grand, and righteous and from blanket solutions to messy, detailed problems. Give us the vision to see that those nations that gave the most to their generals and least to their poor were, throughout all history, the first to fall. Most of all, give us the vision to see that the world is now too dangerous for anything but truth, too small for anything but love. Through Jesus Christ our Lord, who became what we are to make us what he is. Amen.

— *William Sloane Coffin Jr., 1983*

Almighty Lord, God of justice and peace,
we give you thanks on this day
for all those who have given their lives

on behalf of others
who fought for political liberty and human liberty
and to establish international standards
of justice, freedom, and peace.
We give thanks as well
for all those who went forth to serve
and who then returned
to live out their lives in freedom
and for those who in times of conflict
bore witness to the cause of peace.
We ask your forgiveness for the times
when we have failed to bear witness
to the freedom and equality and justice
that we have inherited through the sacrifice of others
and that we too often take for granted
and for the times
when we have misused the power
we have been given
through ignorance, arrogance, or self-righteousness.
Renew this day in our hearts and our lives
the commitment to human freedom and peace
which this day symbolizes
that so we may truly honor those who have died
and bear faithful witness
to the ideals made known to us
and held up before us
by Holy Scriptures, by faithful teachers, pastors, leaders,
and by all those who take their part in the building
of our common life.
Hold up always before us
the vision of the city of peace
and as we struggle to reach it
forgive us our failures,

renew our commitment,
and strengthen us
to serve you
and all those among whom you have placed us:
God of justice,
God of freedom,
God of peace,
Hear our prayer.
Amen.   — *Christopher L. Webber, 2004*

INDEPENDENCE DAY

A Prayer That May Be Used on the Fourth Day of July

O Holy, righteous and immortal God, King of kings and Lord of lords, who dost, from thy heavenly throne behold and govern all the people and kingdoms of this lower world, thou art a strong tower and defence to those who fear and trust in thee; thou art the Giver of all good, and the only hope of all the ends of the earth. With humble adoration we would lift our heart and voice to thee, in praise and prayer. We adore thee as the God in whom our fathers trusted; as the God, whose holy protecting arm has preserved the people of these United States, through many and great perils; has distinguished them by unnumbered blessings, and given them a great name among the nations of the earth. We praise thee for the dispensations of thy bountiful hand, and for all thy goodness vouchsafed to us, thy favoured people.

Through thy blessing, and because thy compassions fail not, we are brought again to behold this anniversary of our national Independence. May its return call to our remembrance thy mercies which have ever been of old; and may we be sensible that not for our own righteousness, or the uprightness of our own heart, hast thou brought us in to possess this good land; nor has the might of our own arm given us victory in battle. Not unto us, O Lord, not unto us, but unto thy name be the praise, for thy mercy and for thy truth's sake.

Grant unto us, we beseech thee, such sense of thy blessings to us, and to the people of our country, that our hearts may be unfeignedly thankful, and our lives be devoted to thee. And we pray, O God, that we and our country may still be under thy holy care and protection. Be thou our shield and our buckler, that we, surely trusting in thy defence, may not fear the power of any adversaries. We beseech thee to continue thy merciful goodness to us and to our country. Give wisdom and strength and union to the government and people of these United States, and this state especially in which we live. Bless all who are set in authority over us, and so enlighten their minds, direct their counsels and strengthen their hands, that righteousness and peace may dwell in our land. May they who are appointed to give laws and to execute them, be endued with wisdom and equity and a just regard to the public good, that, through their impartial ministrations, peace and happiness, truth and justice, religion and piety may increase, and the safety and welfare of thy people be promoted.

Grant, O Lord, that a deep sense of thy providential care may preserve us from pride and self-dependence. While we are thankful for the great blessings of civil liberty, and political independence, may we be preserved from a trust in ourselves, and from all vain confidence of boasting. May we never forget who it is that makes us to differ from others, nor use our liberty for a cloak of maliciousness; but follow after charity and the things which make for peace. Much reason have we to fear that the sins which prevail in our country and our ungrateful returns for thy unnumbered mercies, should provoke thy indignation and call thy judgments upon us. We beseech thee mercifully to look upon our infirmities, and turn from us the evils which we justly have deserved. Preserve us, O Lord, from desolating judgments; from selfishness, discord and contention.

O grant, we beseech thee, that we may be united and happy; ever rejoicing in thy holy protection. And wilt thou, O Lord, be merciful to those, who need the blessings which we enjoy. May light and liberty, and pure and undefiled religion be more and more extended, till all the nations of the earth shall rejoice in thee their God.

And may all who shall assemble on occasion of this anniversary, be duly sensible from whom our blessings flow. Help us to enjoy the bounty which thy hand bestows; with temperance and sobriety, and in thy faith and fear. May this day be so celebrated as not to increase the sins of the nation; but rather, through thy blessing, be so observed as to diffuse the comforts of rational freedom, social affections and pious gratitude throughout the community. Extend thy blessing to our churches; to our religious institutions, and to all our efforts to spread the knowledge of Christ, and the comforts of his gospel. May thy kingdom come, and thy will be done on earth, as it is in heaven. May the days come quickly, when the mountain of the Lord's house shall be established in the top of the mountains, and be exalted above the hills, and all nations flow unto it; when the Redeemer's kingdom shall overspread the earth, and all the ends of the world shall see and rejoice, in the salvation of our God. We ask these things in the name and through the merits of our Lord and Saviour, Jesus Christ. Amen.   — *Alexander Viets Griswold, 1766–1843*

1833: American Independence Day Celebration

O eternal God, through whose mighty power our fathers won their liberties of old; Grant, we beseech thee, that we and all the people of this land may have grace to maintain these liberties in righteousness and peace; through Jesus Christ our Lord. Amen.   — *Book of Common Prayer, 1928*

The following prayer was offered in the United States Senate in the middle of the Second World War.

Our fathers' God and ours, on the birthday of national independence we confess our dependence upon Thee. Without Thee we are lost in spite of the overwhelming might of our national arms.

We thank Thee for those pilgrims of faith who came hither in their frail barque across mountainous seas and who stepped upon strange shores with the salutation to a new world, "In the Name of God. Amen." The Nation here established, conceived in liberty and dedicated to the proposition that all men are created equal has acknowledged that Name above every name and reverenced it, has built its altars, reared its temples, and raised its steeples, emblems of a faith that points to the skies and wings its sure and certain way to God. Make that faith of the fathers, we pray, real to us in these tempestuous days. Save us from a freedom of speech so empty that we have nothing worth saying, from a freedom of worship so futile that we have no God to adore, from freedom from want and fear with no creative idea as to how to use our plenty or our security for the redemption of our social order and for the salvation of our own souls. Let all that is low and unworthy in us sink to the depths. Let all that is high

and fine in us rise to greet the morn of a new day confident
that the best is yet to be. Amen.

— *Frederick Brown Harris, 1943*

O Lord, we praise You
that You have created us for freedom in Your creation,
that You have re-created us for freedom under Your Gospel,
that You enable us to keep Your law in freedom and love.
We confess
we often neglect our rights,
we often abuse our privileges,
we often avoid our obligations.
Keep us
from selfishness that stifles freedom,
from narrow-mindedness that limits freedom,
from hatred that destroys freedom.
Enable people everywhere
to live under free government,
to hear of the freedom of Your Gospel,
to know true freedom in Jesus Christ, our Lord,
in whose name we ask it.
Amen.   — *The Lutheran Book of Prayer, 1970, adapted*

O God, mightily we pray for wisdom, courage, and strength
to serve thee and this nation faithfully in the days that lie
ahead. Remind us of our duty to promote the general welfare, to secure the blessings of liberty for all, to see to it that
justice and compassion reign from sea to shining sea, and
that the bountiful resources of a favored land are not only
thankfully received but also gladly shared with the whole
human family.

We know, O God, that this vision of America has never
been fully realized, but it has never been abandoned. Remind us that it has been significant to the rest of the world,

where echoes and adaptations of it are seen in the revolutions and the constitutions of many nations; it has been a magnet to our own people, charming them away from slavery and sweatshops, chain gangs and lynch mobs, toward broader opportunity, deeper compassion, fuller equality, and greater justice for all. O God, grant wisdom and courage for the living of these days.

Hear too our prayer for those in this congregation and the globe around who are in trouble, sorrow, need, sickness, or any other adversity; may they feel thine everlasting arms. O God, bless this congregation. Bless our worship here today. May thy Holy Spirit be like penetrating oil to loosen the rusted hinges of our hearts, so that we swing wide the doors to thee and to one another. Amen.

— *William Sloane Coffin Jr., 1983*

God, source of all freedom,
this day is bright with the memory
of those who declared that life and liberty
are your gift to every human being.
Help us to continue a good work begun long ago.
Make our vision clear and our will strong:
that only in human solidarity will we find liberty,
and justice only in the honor that belongs
to every life on earth.
Turn our hearts toward the family of nations:
to understand the ways of others,
to offer friendship,
to find safety only in the common good of all.
We ask this through Christ our Lord.

— *Catholic Household Blessings and Prayers, 2007*

LABOR DAY

The First Monday in September

Lord God, our Father and Creator.
We deserve
to labor among thorns and thistles,
to eat by the sweat of our brow,
to work without reward.
For we confess
we have spoiled Your creation by our sin,
we have marred Your work by our neglect,
we have hurt Your work by our rebellion.
We pray You, bless our labor
by Him who was once a carpenter,
by Him who came to be our servant,
by Him who saved us to serve.
For His sake keep us and all who labor
from false dealing and unfair practice,
from excessive profit and unjust gain,
from slovenly service and irrational demands.
Help us
to labor with love,
to labor with joy,
to labor with faithfulness.
Teach us that the best labor we give You
is loving service to others.
In Christ's name we ask it. Amen.
— *The Lutheran Book of Prayer, 1970, adapted*

God our creator,
we are the work of your hands.
Guide us in our work,
that we may do it, not for self alone,

but for the common good.
Make us alert to injustice,
ready to stand in solidarity,
that there may be dignity for all
in labor and in labor's reward.
Grant this through Christ our Lord. Amen.
— *Catholic Household Blessings*
and Prayers, 1988

A Meditation for Labor Day

Creator of all life,
what are you making of us?
Are we working with you in your purpose?
What have we done with our time and energy
to shape our lives toward your purpose?
What have we done with our time and energy
to make a difference in the lives of others?
Redeemer of the world,
you have overcome the limitations of life
and given our lives direction and purpose:
take the things we have done badly
and make of them something better;
take our failures and make them
lessons from which we can learn;
accept our repentance and renew us in your service.
Sanctifier of life,
you make everything holy by your presence;
enable us to see the holiness of life
in the world around us,
hills and trees and streams,
houses and stores and roads,
in the people we meet,
in places where we work;

work through us, we pray, to make your holiness known.
Creator, Redeemer, Sanctifier,
shape our lives in your service;
give us guidance and grace
to work with you toward your purpose
today and tomorrow,
now and always. Amen.   — *Christopher L. Webber, 2005*

ELECTION DAY

Federal elections are set by Congress for the first Tuesday after the first Monday in November. Primary and local elections may occur at other times. Whenever an election occurs, it is an occasion for prayer and recollection that the choices made affect so many others not only in this country but throughout the world. Politicians will often appeal to the individual's self-interest but that should never be the decisive factor for citizens who are conscious of God's will for the people God has created.

At the Time of an Election

Under your law we live, great God,
and by your will we govern ourselves.
Help us as good citizens
to respect neighbors whose views differ from ours,
so that without partisan anger,
we may work out issues that divide us,
and elect candidates to serve the common welfare;
through Jesus Christ the Lord. Amen.

— *The Book of Common Worship,*
Presbyterian Church in the United States
of America, 1946

Before a National Election

Lord Jesus, we ask Thee to guide the people of this nation as they exercise their dearly bought privilege of franchise. May it neither be ignored unthinkingly nor undertaken lightly. As citizens all over this land go to the ballot boxes, give to them a sense of high privilege and joyous responsibility.

Help those who are about to be elected to public office to come to understand the real source of their mandate — a mandate given by no party machine, received at no polling booth, but given by God; a mandate to govern wisely and well; a mandate to represent God and truth at the heart of the nation; a mandate to do good in the name of Him under whom this Republic was established.

We ask Thee to lead America in the paths where Thou wouldst have her walk, to do the tasks which Thou hast laid before her. So may we together seek happiness for all our citizens in the name of Him who created us all equal in His light, and therefore brothers and sisters. Amen.

— Peter Marshall, 1949, adapted

Before an Election

Almighty God, who dost hold us to account for the use of all our powers and privileges; guide us, we pray thee, in the election of our leaders and representatives; that by wise legislation and faithful administration the rights of all may be protected, and our nation enabled to fulfill thy purposes; through Jesus Christ our Lord. Amen.

— Prayers for All Occasions, 1961

At the Time of an Election

O God, who hast created this world of tender beauty which now is laden with such fragile hopes, gratefully we acknowledge that no morning stars that sing together have deeper cause than we for joy, for of thy fullness have we received grace upon grace.

For blue skies filled with rushing clouds, for parks and rivers and neighbors and friends, for the knowledge that there are no more important tragedies than the tragedy of death and no more important victories than the victory of love, God, we praise thy holy name.

And we thank thee for the light streaming from the cross, which discloses not the reasons for pain and injustice (for they remain a mystery), but discloses thee suffering with and for us and by that suffering bringing light and life. O God, that what we know makes bearable what we do not know, that in all ages and lands dark valleys have been turned into havens of light, crosses into shrines, God, for all this we bless thy holy name.

O God, gross darkness now covers the earth and thy people. Come then to thy children, not only as light but also as a consuming fire to set ablaze all the rubbish of the earth: the chauvinism of the nations, the obsolete barriers that sunder those who should be seeing eye to eye and working side by side, the banality of so much of our culture, and the shells and husks, the remnants of our unconsecrated selves. Make us, O God, faithful Christians not only in Galilee but also in Jerusalem. May we seek not to limit the liabilities of our witness, but rather to be loyal and loving to thee and to our neighbors, O loving and faithful Creator of us all. Amen.

— *William Sloane Coffin Jr., 1983*

A Prayer on Election Day

Sovereign Lord, foolish we are, believing that we can rule ourselves by selecting this or that person to rule over us. We are at it again. Help us not to think it more significant than it is, but also give us and those we elect enough wisdom to acknowledge our follies. Help us laugh at ourselves, for without humor our politics cannot be humane. We desire to dominate and thus are dominated. Free us, dear Lord, for otherwise we perish. Amen. — *Stanley Hauerwas, 1999*

Before an Election

Holy God, throughout the ages you have called men and women to serve you in various ways, giving them gifts for the task to which they were called and strengthening and guiding them in the fulfillment of their calling; in this free land you share with us that great responsibility and enable us to choose those who will serve you in positions of leadership in various offices of government.

Help us in so choosing to seek those who have an understanding of your will for us, a commitment to justice, a concern for those in greatest need, a love of truth and a deep humility before you; Send your Spirit among us that we may be guided in the choices we make that so your will may be done on earth as it is in heaven.

— *Christopher L. Webber, 2008*

THANKSGIVING DAY
The Fourth Thursday in November

The custom of a thanksgiving for harvest can be traced back to 1621 when Governor William Bradford proclaimed a day of thanksgiving for the colonists to celebrate a good harvest after a winter of scarcity. It was celebrated as a traditional English harvest feast and the local Wampanoag Indians were invited. Days of thanksgiving were celebrated throughout the colonies after fall harvests at various times until George Washington declared a national holiday in 1789.

In 1863 Abraham Lincoln declared the last Thursday in November a day of thanksgiving and so it remained until Congress passed a joint resolution in 1941 decreeing that Thanksgiving should fall on the fourth Thursday of November, where it remains.

Annual Thanksgiving, 1825

O thou, who art good unto all, who exercisest lovingkindness in all the earth, and who hast come nigh to us by Jesus Christ, thy Son! It is thou who holdest our souls in life; who givest us our daily bread, health in our habitations, peace in our borders, and who crownest the year with thy goodness! We desire this day, with affectionate gratitude, to recount thy mercies, and piously to ascribe honour and blessing, glory and praise to thee, our Rock and Fortress, our Strength and Redeemer. We would rest this day before thee, and make it a season of temperate feasting and religious gladness.

How precious have been thy thoughts unto us, O God! How great is the sum of them! We bless thee for thy smiles upon the year; for the warm influences of the sun; and for timely and. refreshing showers upon our fields. We bless thee for preserving our houses from the ravages of fire; for all the health and pleasures we have enjoyed in them; for every portion of bread which has given strength to our bodies; for whatever has arrested the progress of disease; and for the tear of sympathy which has comforted our trouble. We thank thee for every cheerful sensation, when alone; for the pleasures of friendly intercourse; for the benefits of good neighbourhood; for the privileges of public worship; for the maintenance of civil order; the continuance of peace; the administration of justice; for every encouragement to well-doing; every manifestation of useful truth; and for all the advantages of our condition.

God of goodness! direct us graciously to a right improvement of all thy mercies. Preserve us from the wicked indulgence of all fleshly lusts; and from wasting our substance in riotous living. May we enjoy our earthly possessions with temperance, cheerfulness, and contentment. Protect us against the snares of prosperity. May we honour thee with our substance, be rich in good works, and duly esteem thee, the Rock of our salvation.

Perpetuate our privileges both private and common; continue to us the enjoyment of our civil rights; disappoint the devices of the crafty; prolong the days and usefulness, of those public men under whose administration the righteous flourish, who cause every man to sit without fear under his vine and fig-tree, and who make our land a quiet habitation. O God! grant peace, order, and plenty in our families, our villages, and towns, and throughout our country. May our rulers have wisdom to direct, and integrity to pursue, such plans as shall best promote our highest good. Wilt thou bless all fountains of useful science; heal and cleanse their waters; dispel the mists of ignorance; arrest the progress of profaneness and vice; make the people of our land humble before thee; peaceable in their civil and social relations; and zealous for the establishment of liberty, order, and truth. O may we never, by our ingratitude, incur that censure, "I have nourished and brought up children, but they have rebelled against me."

And now unto the Governor among the nations, on whom their safety and prosperity ultimately depend; unto the King of kings, and Lord of lords, be glory and majesty, dominion and power, forever and ever. Amen

— *A Family Prayer-book, 1825*

A Form of Prayer and Thanksgiving, 1839

Benjamin T. Onderdonk, Bishop of the Episcopal Diocese of New York in 1839, provided this form of prayer and thanksgiving for whatever days of thanksgiving might be appointed by civil authority.

O God, who art the blessed and only Potentate, the King of kings, and Lord of lords; the Almighty Ruler of nations; we adore and magnify Thy glorious name for all the great things which Thou hast done for us. We render Thee thanks for the goodly heritage which Thou hast given us; for the civil and religious privileges which we enjoy; and for the multiplied manifestations of Thy favor toward us. Grant that we may show forth our thankfulness for these Thy mercies, by living in reverence of Thy almighty power and dominion, in humble reliance on Thy goodness and mercy, and in holy obedience to Thy righteous laws.

Preserve, we beseech Thee, to our country, the blessings of peace, restore them to nations deprived of them; and secure them to all the people of the earth. May the kingdom of the Prince of Peace come; and reigning in the hearts and lives of men, unite them in holy fellowship; that so their only strife may be, who shall allow forth, with most humble and holy fervor, the praises of Him who hath loved them, and made them kings and priests unto God.

We implore Thy blessing on all in legislative, judicial, and executive authority, that they may have grace, wisdom, and understanding, so to discharge their duties as most effectually to promote thy glory, the interests of true religion and virtue, and the peace, good order, and welfare of this State and Nation.

Continue, O Lord, to prosper our institutions for the promotion of sound learning, the diffusion of virtuous education, and the advancement of Christian truth, and of the purity and prosperity of Thy Church; change, we beseech Thee, every evil heart of unbelief; and shed the quickening influences of Thy Holy Spirit on all the people of this land.

Save us from the guilt of abusing the blessings of prosperity to luxury and licentiousness, to irreligion and vice; lest we provoke Thee, in just judgment, to visit our offences with a rod, and our sins with scourges. And while Thy unmerited goodness to us, O God of our salvation, leads us to repentance, may we offer ourselves, our souls and bodies, a living sacrifice to Thee, who hast preserved and redeemed us, through Jesus Christ our Lord; on whose merits and mediation alone we humbly rely for the forgiveness of our sins, and the acceptance of our services; and who liveth and reigneth, with the Father and the Holy Ghost, ever one God, world without end. Amen.

A Collect

O Almighty God, who hast never failed those who put their trust in Thee, and dost honor the people who honor Thee; imprint on our hearts, we beseech Thee, a deep and habitual sense of this great truth, that the only security for the continuance of the blessings which we enjoy, consists in our acknowledgment of Thy sovereign and gracious Providence, and in humble and holy submission to the Gospel of Thy Son

Jesus Christ; to whom all power is given in heaven and in earth, and who is one with the Father and the Holy Ghost, in the eternal Godhead, our Mediator and Redeemer. Amen.
— *Benjamin T. Onderdonk, 1839*

O thou Infinite Spirit, who art everywhere that the light of day sheds down its glorious lustre, and in the caverns of the earth where the light of day cometh not, we would draw near to thee and worship thy spirit, which at all times is near to us. O thou Infinite One, who art amidst all the silences of nature, and forsakest us not with thy spirit where the noisy feet of men are continually heard, we pray that the spirit of prayer may be in us while we lift up our hearts unto thee. Thou askest not even our gratitude, but when our cup is filled with blessings to the brim and runneth over with bounties, we would remember thee who fillest it, and givest every good and precious gift.

Father, we thank thee for the special material blessings which we enjoy; for the prosperity which has attended the labors of thy children in the months that are past, for the harvest of corn and of grass which the hand of man, obedient to his toilsome thought, has gathered up from the surface of the ground. We bless thee that when our toil has spoken to the earth, the furrows of the field have answered with sufficient, yea, with abundant returns of harvest to our hand. We thank thee for the blessings of the deep, and treasures hid in the sands, which thy children have gathered. We bless thee for the success which has come to those who go down to the sea in ships and do business in great waters. We thank thee for the treasures which our mining hand has gathered from the foldings of the earth, the wealth which we have quarried from the mountain, or digged out from the bosom of the ground. And we bless thee for the other harvest which from these rude things the toilsome hand and the laborious thought of men have created, turning use into beauty also, and so adorning and gladenning the world.

We thank thee for the special blessings that come near to us this day. We bless thee for the health of our bodies, and thank you for those who are near and dear to us; and for all the gladsome gatherings together which this day will bring to pass, of parents and their children, long severed, or of the lover and his beloved, whoso gladly would become one. We bless thee for all those who this day shall break their bread in common, lifting up their hearts unto thee, and blessing the hand which lengthens out our days and keeps the golden bowl from breaking at the fountain; and we thank thee for those who in many a distant place are still of us, severed in the body, but with us yet in soul.

We remember before thee not only our families and our homes, but likewise the great country in which thou hast cast the lines of our lot. We thank you for its wide extent, for the great riches which the toil of man has gathered together and stored up. We bless thee for the multitudes of people, an exceeding great company of men and women, which here have sprung into existence under thy care. We bless thee that in this land the exile from so many a clime can find a home, with none to molest, nor to make afraid. We thank thee for every good institution which has here been established, for all the truth that is taught in the church, for what of justice has become the common law of the people, and for all of righteousness and of benevolence which goes forth in the midst of our land.

We bless thee for our fathers who in centuries past, in the name of thy holy spirit, and for the sake of rights dearest to mankind, went from one country to another people, and in their day of small things came here. Yea, we thank thee for those whose only communion was an exile, and we bless them for the bravery of their spirit which would not hang the harp on the willow, but sung songs of thanksgiving in a strange land, and in the midst of their wilderness builded a new Zion up, full of thanksgiving and song and praise.

We bless thee for our fathers of a nearer kin, who in a day of peril strove valiantly that they might be free, and bequeathed a noble heritage to their sons and daughters who were to come after them. Yea, we thank thee for those whose sacrament was only a revolution, and the cup of blessing was of blood drawn from their own manly veins; and we bless thee for the hardy valor which drew their swords, and sheathed it not till they had a large place, and their inalienable right secured to them by their own right hand, toiling and striving under the benediction of thy precious providence. Now, Lord, we thank thee that the few have become a multitude, and the little vine which our fathers planted with their tears and watered with their blood, reaches from sea to sea, great clusters of riches hanging on every bough, and its root strong in the land.

But we remember before thee the great sins which this nation has wrought, and while we thank thee for the noblest heritage which man ever inherited from man, we must mourn also that we have blackened the ground with crimes such as seldom a nation has committed against thee. Yea, Lord, even our thanksgiving prayer must be stained with our tears of mourning, and our psalm of thanksgiving must be mingled with the wail of those who lament that they have no hope left for them in the earth. Father, we remember our brothers of our own kin and complexion whom wickedness has smitten down in another land, whose houses are burned and their wives given up to outrage. We remember those who walk only in chains this day, and are persecuted for their righteousness' sake. And still more in our prayer we remember the millions of our brothers whom our fathers chained, and whose fetters our wicked hands have riveted upon their limbs. Lord, we pray thee that we may suffer from these our transgressions, till we learn to eschew evil, to break the rod of the oppressor, and to let the oppressed go free; yea, till we make our rulers righteousness, and those chief amongst us whose glory it is to serve mankind by justice, by fidelity, and by truth.

We pray thee, on this day of our gratitude, that we may rouse up everything that is humanest in our heart, pledging ourselves anew to do justly and to love mercy and to walk humbly before thee, O thou our Father and our Mother on earth and in the heavens too. Thus, Lord, may our thanksgiving be worthy of the nature thou hast given us, and the heritage thou hast bequeathed. Thus may our psalm of gratitude be a hymn of thanksgiving for millions who have broken off their chains, and for a great country full of joy, of blessedness, of freedom and of peace. So may thy kingdom come and thy will be done on earth as it is in heaven.

— *Theodore Parker, November 27, 1856*

Lord, Thou hast indeed been bountiful. As we look back over the years, how gracious Thou hast been, how tender Thy mercy, how warm and constant Thy love.

Create within us, our Father, that true gratitude that shall make this day of Thanksgiving one of rededication, when we shall think not of how much we can eat but of how thankful we ought to be.

So may we — all across this land today — act as recipients of God's richest mercy and bountiful blessing, as we share with others. May we, in gratitude, get on with the job of creating not only a nation but a world in which all people shall have the right to seek happiness.

Help us to make that dream come true in our homes day by day, in street and office and school, and so to live that Thou shalt be able to bless us and bless the nation for which we pray. In His name, who created us a nation, we pray. Amen.

— *Peter Marshall, 1949, adapted*

Eternal God, high and lifted up and yet within us all, with dutiful and adoring awe we come to worship thee. We who through another week have too much looked down on things beneath, would turn our eyes to things above. We, who often have contented ourselves with the things that serve us would now look to the things that have a right to command us. We would be carried out of ourselves by something greater than ourselves to which we give ourselves.

Lift us up, we beseech thee, into the spirit of adoration. Help us to see in life whatever is excellent and beautiful, august and of good report, that we may be no longer disillusioned and dismayed before the ugliness of life but may renew our confidence in God and godliness.

Lift us up into the spirit of thanksgiving. Quicken our sense of gratitude. If in the unending conversation within our minds we have spoken to ourselves only about our difficulties and our ills, help us to remember this day the benedictions that have made life beautiful and the blessings through which thou hast shined upon us. Recall to our thought our friends, the homes that have nourished us, the people who have loved us, great books, great music, great art, those who in sacrifice laid the foundations of the social securities which we enjoy. Make real to us Him who loved us and gave Himself for us, and so elevate our worship, we beseech thee, until it is a festival. Help us to celebrate our God this day in the spirit of thanksgiving.

Lift us up, we beseech thee, into the spirit of confession. Forgive us for the carelessness with which we regard those sins that hurt, not ourselves alone, but other lives as well. Teach us afresh that we cannot sin unto ourselves but that every evil grudge we harbor and every vindictive wish we cherish and every unkind, unclean thing we do is like poison given to our friends. Deepen within us, therefore, we beseech thee, our conscientiousness. Help us this day, with a fine sense of honor, honestly to face our own souls and to say before thee and one another, We have sinned.

Lift us up, we beseech thee, into the spirit of intercession. Save us from the narrowness of our sympathies. Keep us, we beseech thee, from our provinciality. Widen the borders of our understanding and our care. If we are prosperous, bring to our hearts the thought of the poor; if we are well, the sick; if we are happy, the sorrowful; if our family circles are unbroken, the bereaved; and help us in such sincerity to pray that we may go out to work and make our hearts and hands a channel through which the care of God can flow down into some unhappy life.

Lift us up, we beseech thee, to a higher thought about our country. In these feverish days, save us from being feverish. Give this country, we beseech thee, a finer spirit, a saner wisdom, and increased goodwill. Forbid us from our bigotry and our intolerance. Give us the grace of strong convictions joined with a sympathetic understanding of those who differ from us. Let wisdom be deepened in our commonwealth, that the great business which as a nation we have on hand may be wrought out in soberness and truth as becomes the children of our forebears.

Lift up our spirit into intercession for the church. Forgive it for its infidelity to its Lord. Forgive us the contrast between Christianity and Christ. He is so great; we are so unworthy.

Upon all thy people everywhere, who in sincerity and truth, working in the spirit of Jesus, are lifting the levels of our human life closer to oneness, righteousness, and peace, let thy benediction fall! Across the barriers that we have made, the sectarian lines that we have named, we pray unto the God who has said, "All souls are mine." Save us from our narrowness into thy breadth. Save us from our littleness to thy universality. O God, who art great, make us great also in our love.

And now, beyond the power of our small words to carry the needs of thy people here, do thou cross the inner thresholds of our hearts and minister not according to our desert but according to the riches of thy grace in Christ Jesus, our Lord. Amen.   — *Harry Emerson Fosdick, 1983*

> Heavenly Father,
> from whom come all good and perfect gifts,
> from whom come mercies new each day,
> from whom come blessings beyond measure:
> Accept our thanksgiving
> for protection and those who provide it,
> for daily bread and those who prepare it,
> for clothing and those who manufacture it,
> for family and those dear to us,
> for friends and those associated with us,
> for jobs and those working with us,
> for social security and support programs.
> We confess we think too little
> about the fact that we deserve nothing,
> about the many who serve us,
> about the blessings of Your Spirit,
> We pray You,
> forgive our ingratitude,
> open our eyes to behold Your goodness,

fill our hearts with thankfulness,
make us respond in appreciation,
help us to serve in love.
We thank You; through Christ, our Lord,
Your best gift to us. Amen.
— *The Lutheran Book of Prayer, 1970*

God of the universe, creative Source of all being, from You come our blessings from day to day and from year to year. How great are your love and kindness, O God! The towering mountains and the shaded forests, the abundant streams and the fruitful earth Your endless bounty.

For this land so richly blessed, we raise our voices in joyous thanks. To these shores Your children have come from many lands to seek liberty and new hope. All have been pilgrims to this western world. Though they did not always practice the justice they sought, here they found renewed purpose, increased strength, and the opportunity to outgrow old fears and superstitions. For our country, for its freedom promised and attained, for the richness of its natural blessing, and for the growing harmony of its citizens, we give humble thanks.

O God of justice and right, inspire all who dwell in our beloved land with loyalty to the ideals of its founders. Give us wisdom and strength to labor for its well-being, on the firm foundation of justice and truth. Fill us with the spirit of kindness, generosity, and peace, that this land may be a beacon-light to many people.

We Give Thanks This Day

For the expanding grandeur of Creation, worlds known and unknown, galaxies beyond galaxies, filling us with awe; challenging our imaginations:

We give thanks this day.

For this fragile planet earth, its times and tides, its sunsets and seasons:

We give thanks this day.

For the joy of human life, its wonders and surprises, its hopes and achievements:

We give thanks this day.

For our human community, our common past, and future hope, our oneness transcending all separation, our capacity to work for peace and justice in the midst of hostility and oppression:

We give thanks this day.

For high hopes and noble causes, for faith without fanaticism, for understanding of views not shared:

We give thanks this day.

For all who have labored and suffered for a fairer world, who have lived so that others might live in dignity and freedom:

We give thanks this day.

For human liberty and sacred rites; for opportunities to change and grow, to affirm and choose:

We give thanks this day.

We pray that we may not live by our fears but by our hopes, not by our words but by our deeds.

The Heavens Declare the Glory of God

How wonderful, O God, are the works of Your hands! The heavens declare Your glory. The arch of sky displays Your handiwork:

The heavens declare the Glory of God.

In your love, You have given us the power to behold the beauty of Your world, robed in all its splendor. The sun and the stars, the valleys and the hills, the rivers and lakes: All disclose Your presence:

The earth reveals God's Eternal Presence.

— *Union Prayer Book I — Sinai Edition, 2000*

Lord, we thank you
for the goodness of our people
and for the spirit of justice
that fills this nation.
We thank you for the beauty and fullness of the land
and the challenge of the cities.
We thank you for our work and our rest,
for one another, and for our homes.
We thank you, Lord:
accept our thanksgiving on this day.
We pray and give thanks through Jesus Christ our
Lord. Amen.

— *Catholic Household Blessings and Prayers, 2007*

About the Authors

Henry Ward Beecher (1813–1887) was pastor of the Plymouth Congregational Church in Brooklyn for forty years and a leading voice for abolition and liberal causes.

Walter Russell Bowie (1882–1969), a graduate of Harvard University and the Virginia Theological Seminary, served as a hospital chaplain in France during World War I and as Professor of Practical Theology at Union Theological Seminary from 1939. He is probably best known as the author of the hymn "Lord Christ, When First Thou Cam'st to Men" (1928).

Malcolm Boyd (1923–) is an Episcopal priest, whose book *Are Your Running with Me, Jesus?* (1965) pioneered a modern and informal style of prayer that attracted wide attention and helped move English-speaking Christians away from a heavy reliance on seventeenth-century language.

Charles Henry Brent (1862–1929) was a leader in the ecumenical movement, a missionary, a bishop of the Episcopal Church, and a chaplain with the American Expeditionary Force in World War I.

Margaret Bullitt-Jonas (1951–) is a graduate of Harvard University and the Episcopal Divinity School. She has served parishes in the Diocese of Massachusetts and written a number of books on spiritual growth.

Consecrated in 1790, *John Carroll* (1735–1815) was the first Roman Catholic bishop in the United States and is considered to be one of those responsible for the first amendment to the Constitution. When George Washington died, Carroll directed his clergy to observe February 22 as a day of mourning.

John Coburn (1914–) served as Dean of the Episcopal Divinity School, President of the House of Deputies of General Convention, Bishop of Massachusetts, and is the author of several books including a collection of prayers.

William Sloane Coffin Jr. (1924–2006) was a liberal Christian clergyman and long-time peace activist with international stature. He was ordained in the Presbyterian Church and later received ministerial standing in the United Church of Christ. He served as Chaplain at Yale University and later as Senior Minister at the Riverside Church in New York City.

Germaine Griffin Copeland is the founder and president of Word Ministries, Inc. located in Monroe, Georgia. She also served as the Pastor of Word of Life Church in Smyrna, Georgia.

Henry N. Couden (1843–1922), blinded by a Civil War injury, was educated at the Ohio State School for the Blind and the Divinity School of St. Lawrence University. A Universalist pastor, he served as Chaplain to the House of Representatives from 1895 to 1922

A. Powell Davies (1902–1957), born in England of Welsh parents, became an American citizen in 1935 and served congregations in Maine and New Jersey before becoming minister of All Souls Church in Washington, D.C., where he served from 1944 to 1957. A leading voice in the tradition of liberal Christianity, he said, "Prayer goes on where other language leaves off."

Willie Davis (1937–) was pastor of the Second Baptist Church, Las Vegas, Nevada, and served as Guest Chaplain in the House of Representatives in March 2003.

Stephen Elliott (1806–1866) was Bishop of the Episcopal Diocese of Georgia from 1841 to 1866 and served as Presiding Bishop of the Episcopal Church in the Confederate States.

James A. Forbes Jr. (1935–) served congregations in Virginia and North Carolina before becoming professor of preaching at Union Seminary. He served as Pastor of the Riverside Church, New York, from 1989 to 2007.

Harry Emerson Fosdick (1878–1969) served both Baptist and Presbyterian churches but was best known as the pastor of the Riverside Church in New York, which was built for him with generous donations from John D. Rockefeller. He served there from the time the building was completed in 1930 until his retirement in 1945.

Campbell Gillon (1927–) served for twenty-seven years in the Church of Scotland and then for twenty-three years was pastor of the Georgetown Presbyterian Church. He was Guest Chaplain in the United States Senate in March of 2003.

William (Billy) Graham (1918–) was a leading twentieth-century evangelist who took part in the inauguration ceremonies of seven consecutive American presidents.

The descendant of a long line of New England Congregation-alists, *Alexander Viets Griswold* (1766–1843) was influenced by his uncle, the one Anglican in the family, and studied privately for ordination. After serving three small parishes in northern Connecticut for nine years, Griswold became Rector of the Church in Bristol, Rhode Island, and in 1810 was chosen to serve as bishop of the four dioceses of northern New England. Though he rejected the call at first, he was finally persuaded to accept it and served as bishop of what was called "the Eastern Diocese" for thirty-three years, visiting his far-flung parishes annually and encouraging, in spite of the weakened condition of American churches, support for foreign missions.

Frank T. Griswold (1937–) served as Bishop of the Diocese of Chicago and then as the Presiding Bishop of the Episcopal Church from 1998 to 2007.

Edward Everett Hale (1822–1909) was author of the famous short story "The Man without a Country" and over sixty books on a range of subjects, and pastor of the South Congregational Church in Boston from 1856–1899. Deeply involved in the cause of abolition and efforts for popular education such as the Chautauqua movement, he was honored by a six-month appointment as Chaplain of the United States Senate in 1903. His prayers, always extemporaneous, were recorded by the Stenographic Recorders of the Senate.

Frederick Brown Harris (1890–1970) was a Methodist minister and fifty-sixth Chaplain of the U.S. Senate, 1942–1947, 1949–1969, serving in that capacity longer than anyone else in history.

Stanley Hauerwas (1940–) is a Methodist theologian and professor of law who has taught at the University of Notre

Dame and is currently Professor of Theological Ethics at Duke Divinity School. He is a pacifist and advocate of non-violence, who argues that nationalism, particularly American patriotism, has no place in the Church. In 2001, *TIME* magazine named him "America's Best Theologian."

John Heuss (1908–1966) was an Episcopal priest who served St. Matthew's Church, Evanston, Illinois, from 1937 to 1947 and then became Director of the Department of Christian Education at the National Council of the Episcopal Church from 1947 to 1952. He was Rector of Trinity Parish, Wall Street, from 1952 to 1966.

John Henry Hobart (1775–1830) was the third bishop of the Episcopal Diocese of New York and a central figure in the revival of the Episcopal Church after the American Revolution.

Walter Quarrier Hullihen (1841–1923) was twenty years old when the American Civil War began and he served under General J. E. B. Stuart, one of the leading generals in that conflict. After the war, he graduated from the Virginia Theological Seminary, was ordained in 1868, and became Rector of Trinity Church, Staunton, Virginia, where he served until his death in 1923.

Born in slavery, *Absalom Jones* (1746–1818) educated himself and purchased first his wife's freedom and then his own. The first African American ordained in the Episcopal Church, Jones formed a congregation that was admitted to the Diocese of Pennsylvania in 1794 and became St. Thomas African Episcopal Church. In the Yellow Fever epidemic of 1794, he organized volunteers when the mayor called for help to bury the dead. It is said of him that, "His piety, pastoral faithfulness, and moral integrity were legendary."

Martin Luther King Jr. (1929–1968) was an African American Baptist pastor who gained prominence through his leadership of a civil rights protest in Birmingham, Alabama, and became the chief spokesperson of the nonviolent civil rights movement. He was assassinated in 1968.

Isidore Lewinthal (1850–1922) was rabbi of Temple Ohabai Sholom, Vine Street, Nashville, Tennessee, from 1888 to 1922.

George Lyman Locke (1835–1919), was an Episcopal priest who served for forty-two years as Rector of St. Michael's Church, Bristol, Rhode Island. His "Prayer for our Country" is one of the most widely known of all prayers for America and appears in various versions in a number of prayer books — including that of the Anglican Church of Nigeria.

Thomas Merton (1915–1968) was one of the most influential Roman Catholic authors of the twentieth century. A Trappist monk, popular spiritual writer, and social activist, Merton was also an advocate of inter-faith dialogue.

Lloyd John Ogilvie (1930–) was Pastor of First Presbyterian Church, Hollywood, California, from 1972 to 1995 and Chaplain of the United States Senate from 1995 to 2003.

Benjamin Treadwell Onderdonk (1791–1861) served as the Bishop of the Episcopal Diocese of New York from 1830 to 1861.

A liberal in religion and politics, *Theodore Parker* (1810–1860) questioned the authority of the Bible and supported the abolition of slavery, even justifying the killing of slave owners by their slaves. His views offended many but his supporters organized a Congregational Church for him in Boston and it drew seven thousand members.

Ze Barney Thorne Phillips (1875–1942) served as Chaplain to the United States Senate through the first two terms of Franklin Roosevelt's presidency. He earned degrees from Wittenberg College and studied for two years at Oxford before his ordination to the priesthood in 1900. He then served parishes in Ohio, Illinois, Missouri, and Pennsylvania before becoming Rector of the Church of the Epiphany in Washington, D.C., in 1924.

A professor of mathematics and philosophy at Union College before being ordained, *Alonzo Potter* (1800–1865) served as Rector of St. Paul's, Boston, and then as vice-president of Union College before being elected Bishop of Pennsylvania in 1845. He founded the Philadelphia Divinity School (now merged with the Episcopal Divinity School in Cambridge, Massachusetts) and worked for temperance reform and the abolition of slavery.

Henry Codman Potter (1835–1908) was educated at the Virginia Theological Seminary and served parishes in Pennsylvania, New York, and Boston before becoming Rector of Grace Church, Manhattan. In his sixteen years there (1868–1894) he worked to create an "institutional church" with day nurseries, kindergartens, and clubs for working people. He was made assistant bishop of New York in 1868 and Diocesan Bishop in 1887. As bishop he attacked the corrupt city government and was deeply involved in inner city mission and in working to resolve labor disputes.

Horatio Potter (1802–1887) was professor of mathematics and natural philosophy at Washington College (now Trinity College), Hartford, Connecticut, before becoming Rector of St. Peter's Church, Albany, New York, and then serving as bishop in the Diocese of New York from 1854 to 1887.

Walter Rauschenbusch (1861–1918) was a Baptist minister who became a leading voice in the "Social Gospel" at the end of the nineteenth and beginning of the twentieth century. In *Christianity and the Social Crisis* (1907) and his other writings he spoke of the importance of society's responsibility rather than the individual's responsibility.

William Rogers (1751–1824) was the first student at Rhode Island College (now Brown University), became Pastor of the First Baptist Church of Philadelphia, and served as a military chaplain during the American Revolution. He was Professor of Oratory and the English Language at the University of Philadelphia (now Pennsylvania) from 1789 to 1811.

Franklin D. Roosevelt (1882–1945), the thirty-second President of the United States, wrote the D-Day prayer and released it to the newspapers in advance with the request that Americans read it with him when he spoke on the radio to announce the invasion of Europe.

Samuel Seabury (1729–1796) studied medicine in Scotland before being ordained and returning to America as a missionary for the Society for the Propagation of the Gospel. He served as a chaplain to the British forces during the Revolution but afterward was chosen by the clergy of Connecticut to go to Scotland and be consecrated as the first bishop in the western hemisphere. Many of his surviving prayers are found in the journal which he kept on his travels from parish to parish as a bishop.

Matthew Simpson (1811–1884) was bishop of the Methodist Episcopal Church and a close personal friend of Abraham Lincoln, who looked to him for advice on the basis of his extensive travel and familiarity with public opinion.

Charles Lewis Slattery (1867–1930) was Rector of Grace Church Manhattan before being elected Bishop Coadjutor of Massachusetts in 1922. He served as Bishop of the Diocese from 1927 to 1930.

Byron Sunderland (1819–1901) served for forty-five years as Pastor of the First Presbyterian Church in Washington, D.C., and served as Chaplain of the United States Senate from 1861 to 1864 and from 1873 to 1878. From 1867 to 1869 he served also as President of Howard University.

Louis J. Swichkow (1916–2007) served as the Rabbi of Beth El Ner Tamid Synagogue in Milwaukee, Wisconsin, for nearly fifty years.

Sayyid M. Syeed (1935–), born in Karachi, is a naturalized U.S. citizen, earned a doctorate in sociolinguistics from Indiana University, Bloomington, and is Secretary General of the Islamic Society of North America.

George Thomas was Minister of Outreach and Institutional Relations from 1977 to 1983 at the Riverside Church, New York.

Howard Thurman (1899–1981) was born in Florida and educated at Morehouse College, Rochester Theological Seminary, and Haverford College before being ordained in the Baptist Church. He served as pastor of a Baptist church in Oberlin, Ohio, and then on the faculties of Morehouse and Spelman colleges in Atlanta, Howard University in Washington, and Boston University. He was an important influence on Martin Luther King Jr. and *Life* magazine named him one of the twelve great preachers of the twentieth century.

Siraj Wahhaj was Imam of Masjid al-Taqwa in Brooklyn, a member of the advisory board of the Islamic Society of

North America, and a member of the board of directors of the American Muslim Council in Washington, D.C.

Christopher L. Webber (1932–) is a graduate of Princeton University and the General Theological Seminary (STB, STM, DD) and the author of a number of books and hymns. He served inner city, suburban, overseas, and rural parishes as an Episcopal priest.

William White (1747–1836) was born in Philadelphia and ordained in England at the age of twenty-five. Returning to the United States, he became the assistant at Christ Church in his native city and, becoming Rector seven years later, continued to serve that parish until his death sixty-four years later. He served as Chaplain of the Continental Congress from 1777 to 1789 and as Chaplain of the United States Senate until 1800. Consecrated a bishop in 1787, he served as the Presiding Bishop of the Episcopal Church at the first General Convention in 1789 and then from 1795 until his death.

Smallwood Edmond Williams (1907–1991) was a leading Pentecostal preacher and Presiding Bishop of the Bible Way Church of Our Lord Jesus Christ.

Bibliography

Prayer Books and Collections

The Book of Common Worship. Presbyterian Church in the United States of America, 1946.

Book of Common Worship. Louisville: Westminster John Knox Press, 1993.

Book of Worship. New York: United Church of Christ, 1986.

Catholic Household Blessings and Prayers. Bishops' Committee on the Liturgy, National Conference of Catholic Bishops. Washington, D.C.: United States Catholic Conference, Inc., 1988.

The Congressional Record. Prayers of the Senate and House Chaplains can be found in the *Congressional Record* for the dates indicated.

A Family Prayer-book: Containing Forms of Morning and Evening Prayers, for a Fortnight. With Those for Schools, Religious Societies, and Individuals. Boston: Cummings, Hilliard & Co., 1825.

A Form of Prayer issued By Special Command of his Majesty George III Imploring Divine assistance against the King's unhappy deluded Subjects in America now in rebellion against the Crown. London 1776; reproduced in facsimile Julius F. Sachse, Philadelphia, 1898.

179

Gates of the House: The New Union Home Prayer Book; Prayers and Readings for Home and Synagogue. Central Conference of American Rabbis, 1977.

The Lutheran Book of Prayer. St. Louis: Concordia Publishing House, 1970.

The Moravian Book of Worship. Bethlehem, Pa.: Moravian Church in America, 1995.

The New Worship Handbook. Cincinnati: Forward Movement Publications, 1966.

Prayers for All Occasions. Cincinnati: Forward Movement Publications, 1961.

The Services of the Protestant Episcopal Church in the United States of America as Ordered by the Bishops during the Civil War. Brooklyn, 1864.

Union Prayer Book I, Sinai Edition. Chicago: Chicago Sinai Congregation, 2000.

The Worshipbook: Services and Hymns. Prepared by the Joint Committee on Worship for Cumberland Presbyterian Church / Presbyterian Church in the United States / The United Presbyterian Church in the United States of America. Philadelphia: Westminster Press, 1975.

Individual Authors

Beecher, Henry Ward. *Prayers from Plymouth Pulpit.* New York: C. Scribner & Company, 1867.

Boyd, Malcolm. *Running with Jesus: The Prayers of Malcolm Boyd.* Minneapolis: Augsburg, 2000.

Brent, Charles Henry. *Adventures in Prayer.* New York: Harper, 1932.

Bullitt-Jonas, Margaret, in *Women's Uncommon Prayers,* ed. Elizabeth Rankin Geitz, Marjorie A. Burke, Ann Smith, and Debra Q. Bennett. Harrisburg, Pa.: Morehouse Publishing, 2000.

Coburn, John B. *A Diary of Prayers, Personal and Public.* Philadelphia: Westminster Press, 1975.

Copeland, Germaine. *Prayers That Avail Much.* Tulsa, Okla.: Harrison House, 1997.

Davies, A. Powell. *The Language of the Heart.* Washington, D.C.: All Soul's Church, Unitarian, 1956.

DeMar, Gary. *God and Government: A Biblical and Historical Study.* Atlanta: American Vision Press, 1982.

Elliott, Stephen. *How to Renew Our National Strength, A Sermon preached in Christ Church Savannah, on Friday, November 15th, 1861, being the day of Humiliation, Fasting, and Prayer, appointed by the President of the Confederate States.* Savannah, Georgia: Steam Power Press of John M. Cooper & Co., 1861.

Forbes, James, "O God of Love, Power and Justice." Unpublished, 1990.

Graham, William. Inauguration Prayers are available online at *www.wheaton.edu/bgc/archives/inaugural.*

Gray, Edward McQueen. *A Nation's Prayer.* Florence, N.M.: Alamo Publishing Office, 1898.

Hale, Edward Everett. *Prayers in the Senate. Prayers offered in the Senate of the United States in the winter session of 1904.* Boston: Little, Brown, and Company, 1904.

Hauerwas, Stanley. *Prayers Plainly Spoken.* Eugene, Ore.: Wipf and Stock, 1999.

Heuss, John. *A Book of Prayers.* New York: Morehouse-Gorham Company, 1957.

Hobart, John Henry. *A form of prayer and thanksgiving to be used in the congregations of the Protestant Episcopal Church in the state of New-York, on the second Thursday in April, A.D. 1815 : being the day appointed by the President of the United States, and the Governor of the state of New-York, as a day of thanksgiving to almighty God for the various public mercies of his providence, and especially for the restoration of the blessings of peace.* New York: T. and J. Swords, 1815.

Jones, Absalom. *Thanksgiving Sermon, Preached January 1, 1808, in St. Thomas' Church, or the African Episcopal Church, Philadelphia: on Account of the Abolition of the African Slave Trade on that day by the Congress of the United States.* Philadelphia, 1808.

King, Martin Luther, Jr., as quoted in *Hymns of Universal Praise.* Hong Kong: Chinese Christian Literature Council, 2006.

Marshall, Peter. *The Prayers of Peter Marshall.* Ed. Catherine Marshall. New York: McGraw-Hill Book Company, 1949.

Merton, Thomas. *Congressional Record,* April 18, 1962.

Moore, Paul Jr. *Will the Bishop Pray? Prayers and Benedictions at Yale University by the Right Reverend Paul Moore Jr., Fellow of the Yale Corporation, 1964–1990, published on the occasion of his retirement.* New Haven, Conn.: Yale University Press, 1991.

Nash, Henry Sylvester. *Prayers and Meditations.* New York: Longmans, Green, and Co., 1915.

Parker, Theodore. *Prayers.* Boston: Roberts Brothers, 1882.

Potter, Henry Codman. *Prayers for Priest and People.*

Rainsley, Glen E. *Words of Worship: Resources for Church and Home.* New York: Pilgrim Press, 1991.

Rauschenbusch, Walter. *For God and the People: Prayers of the Social Awakening.* New York: Pilgrim Press, 1910.

Rogers, William. *An Oration in Commemoration of the Independence of the United States of North America, Delivered*

July 4, 1787, at the Reformed Calvinist Church in Philadelphia by James Campbell, Esquire, to which is prefixed an Introductory Prayer Delivered on the Same Occasion by the Rev. William Rogers. Philadelphia: Pritchard and Hall, 1787.

Seabury, Samuel, "A Prayer for the Courts of Justice." Early American Imprints, First Series, no. 47.

Slattery, Charles Lewis. *Prayers for Private and Family Use.* New York: Macmillan, 1922

Suter, John Wallace. *Prayers for a New World.* New York: Charles Scribner's Sons, 1964.

Swichkow, Louis. *Invocations.* New York: Bloch Publishing Co., 1964.

Thorne, Leo S. *Prayers from Riverside.* New York: Pilgrim Press, 1983 (includes prayers written by Harry Emerson Fosdick, Robert McCracken, George Thomas, and William Sloane Coffin Jr.).

Thurman, Howard. *Meditations of the Heart.* Richmond, Ind.: Friends United Press, 1976.

Williams, Smallwood Edmond. *Significant Sermons.* Washington, D.C.: Bible Way Church, 1970.

Acknowledgments
and Permissions

Every effort has been made to trace the copyright owners of material included in this book. The author and publishers would be grateful if any omission or inaccuracies in these acknowledgments could be brought to their attention for correction in any future edition.

Permission has been received to use material from the following:

The Liturgical Conference: A Prayer for Martin Luther King's birthday

The United States National Conference of Catholic Bishops for permission to use material from *Catholic Household Blessings and Prayers,* Bishops' Committee on the Liturgy, 1988.

Beacon Press for permission to use material from Howard Thurman, *Meditations of the Heart*. Richmond, Ind.: Friends United Press, 1976.

Bloch Publishing Co. for permission to use material from Louis Swichkow, *Invocations*.

Malcolm Boyd, for permission to use material from *Running with Jesus: The Prayers of Malcolm Boyd.*

Chicago Sinai Congregation for permission to use material from *Union Prayer Book I, Sinai Edition.*

Church Publishing for permission to use material from John Heuss, *A Book of Prayers* and Margaret Bullitt-Jonas, in *Women's Uncommon Prayers.*

Concordia Publishing House for permission to use material from *The Lutheran Book of Prayer.*

Forward Movement Publications for permission to use material from *The New Worship Handbook* and *Prayers for All Occasions.*

Harrison House, Tulsa, Oklahoma, for permission to use material from Germaine Copeland, *Prayers That Avail Much.* © 1997.

Mrs. A. Powell Davies for permission to use material from A. Powell Davies, *The Language of the Heart.*

The Pilgrim Press for permission to use material from Leo S. Thorne, *Prayers from Riverside,* and Glen E. Rainsley, *Words of Worship: Resources for Church and Home.* New York.

The Westminster John Knox Press for permission to use material from *The Worshipbook: Services and Hymns* © 1970, 1972, and *The Book of Common Worship, 1993,* and *The Book of Common Worship,* 1946.

Wipf and Stock, Publishers for permission to use material from Stanley Hauerwas, *Prayers Plainly Spoken.*